Southern Living®
everyday
gardening

ISBN-13: 978-0-8487-3352-0
ISBN-10: 0-8487-3352-5
Library of Congress Number: 2010925168

Oxmoor House, Inc.
VP, Publishing Director: Jim Childs
Editorial Director: Susan Payne Dobbs
Brand Manager: Daniel Fagan
Senior Editor: Rebecca Brennan
Managing Editor: Laurie S. Herr

Southern Living Everyday Gardening
Editor: Susan Ray
Project Editor: Holly D. Smith
Senior Designer: Melissa Jones Clark
Senior Production Manager: Greg Amason

Contributors
Writer: Dawn Cannon
Copy Editor: Jasmine Hodges
Proofreader: Donna Baldone
Interns: Christine Taylor Boatright, Caitlin Watzke
Indexer: Mary Ann Laurens

Southern Living:
Executive Editor: Derick Belden
Garden Editor: Gene B. Bussell
Senior Writer: Stephen P. Bender
Associate Garden Editor: Rebecca Bull Reed
Senior Photographers: Ralph Anderson, Van Chaplin, Gary Clark,
Jennifer Davick, Art Meripol
Photographers: Robbie Caponetto, Laurey W. Glenn, Beth Dreiling Hontzas
Production Services Photo Coordinator: Ginny P. Allen
Production Coordinator: Paula Dennis

To order additional publications, call 1-800-765-6400 or 1-800-491-0551

For more books to enrich your life, visit oxmoorhouse.com

Southern Living®

everyday gardening

smart design • simple landscape ideas
best plants and flowers

Oxmoor
House®

contents

Welcome

This book is designed to give you the confidence to transform your yard into a beautiful retreat. We've broken the parts of a great garden—design, elements, plants, and essential information—into chapters to guide and inspire you.

Everyday Gardening opens with a chapter that features 10 great examples of beautiful Southern gardens. We highlight some of our favorite features and neat details to show you how plants, structures, and outdoor furnishings work together to create inviting and comfortable garden spaces.

Keep in mind that gardens are so much more than plants. They rely on structures for shape and dimension. Turn to page 66 to discover key elements to use in the landscape, such as arbors, patios, decks, fences, and even outdoor fireplaces.

Once you've established a plan, add texture, form, and color with plants. The gardens we visit each year—whether grand, formal designs or small cottage gardens—never cease to amaze us with their skillful combinations of plants. Plants are the decoration in a garden, but like all living things, they have certain requirements to flourish. Beginning on page 102, you'll discover some of the best choices for your garden, along with helpful tips to ensure that they grow and thrive.

Kitchen and vegetable gardens offer an opportunity to turn a tiny corner or a wide swath of your yard into a personal produce market. Certain plants and vegetables are particularly suited to various regions. Find out how to successfully bring just-picked goodness from your garden to your kitchen with the special tips beginning on page 196.

A how-to section starting on page 234 breaks down garden tasks to provide you with the must-know essentials for planting, watering, pruning, and fertilizing. The monthly checklists beginning on page 249 will help you keep your garden in top shape all year long.

Turn the page and discover how easy it is to have a beautiful Southern yard to enjoy year-round.

Derick Belden, Executive Editor

design your garden

Great gardens start with a great design. Before you turn
the first patch of dirt or plant the first plant, plan your
garden's layout. This chapter showcases 10 very different
gardens from across the South to inspire you and help you
get started. Enjoy!

Front Yard Face-lift

Creating a first impression with your garden is important.
These home-owners added a fence, walk, and flowers to an already
charming cottage, elevating it to the best house on the block.

'Peggy Martin' rose

Make your entry garden special—it's the first thing that greets guests.

Even natural beauties can use a little lipstick. This Lafayette, Louisiana, home designed by famed architect A. Hays Town features a deep porch, perfect for whiling away an afternoon. However, naked beds and a yard that stretched to the street were less than inviting. Landscape architect Ted Viator and homeowner Joretta Chance made some clever changes that added a warm and welcoming look to the classic design of the house.

Frame the front. It might seem counterintuitive to fence a small yard, but it actually adds an extra layer of dimension, making the yard seem larger.
Welcome with flowers. Put your best foot forward by adding color to the front. Go for layers of climbing roses, annuals, and perennials for a long-lasting show.

Start With the Basics

It's tempting to dive right in with pretty flowers and foliage, but getting the framework right makes all the difference.

Add a new fence. The house is only about 30 feet from the street, so when Joretta sat on the porch, she felt like she was on display. A 42-inch-high iron fence, set 6 feet from the street, runs along the front of the yard and lends privacy and separation. Opting for an iron fence rather than a solid one gives the yard an open, more welcoming feel.

Create a new walk. To lead guests from the street, Ted installed a new brick walk outside the fence. The new walk is the perfect spot for conversing with neighbors. "It's also much more convenient for people who park their cars on the street to step out onto brick rather than grass," says Joretta. Its generous 5-foot width allows guests to walk side by side. To tie the new walk in with the house, Ted chose the same type of brick used on the porch and the existing walk. The running bond pattern

Before

design defined

Start with the hardscape. Fences and walks add structure and framework to the garden. **Why it works:** The low, open fence frames the yard and offers some privacy for the porch without blocking views. The new walk makes it easier for guests to park on the street and approach the front door.

Repeat materials for a cohesive look. Choosing the same type of brick used on the existing porch and walk helps the new walk blend seamlessly. **Why it works:** The addition complements rather than competes with the traditional style of the house.

Choose the right plants. A mix of annuals and perennials provides color from spring into fall. Old-fashioned pass-along plants give the garden a sense of history. **Why it works:** Blooms greet passersby for months out of the year. Pass-along plants have proven their mettle and are great to share with neighbors and friends.

(rows of brick laid in the same direction) also mimics the existing brick.

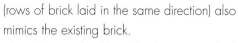
Plant flowers that flourish. Plantings on both sides of the fence make for a pretty view, coming and going. Traditional Southern flowers such as climbing rose, blue and white agapanthus, and petunias win top billing. "Often, old-fashioned plants have proved themselves better than new hybrids," says Ted. Among Joretta's favorite roses is 'Peggy Martin,' a pink thornless climber that survived Hurricane Katrina.

'Gertrude Jekyll' rose.

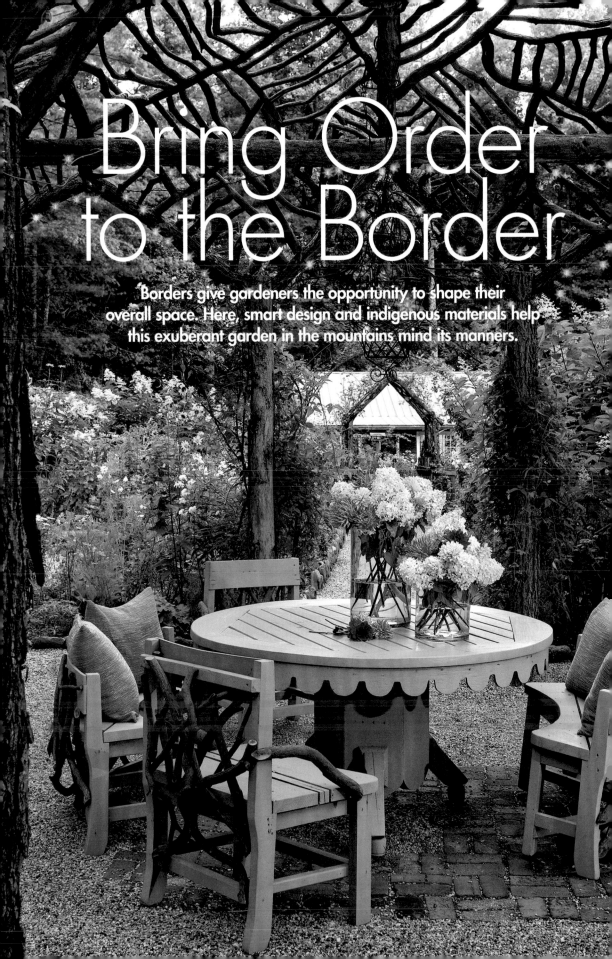

Bring Order to the Border

Borders give gardeners the opportunity to shape their overall space. Here, smart design and indigenous materials help this exuberant garden in the mountains mind its manners.

Add structure to the garden to give it form and keep it neat.

Mother Nature has a tendency to run wild if you let her. In the mountains of North Carolina, Fred Hirons and his late wife, Marty, gave their garden an education in proper manners. Drawing inspiration from classic European gardens, the couple used geometric beds and perpendicular pathways to rein in plantings and give the landscape an English accent.

Native timber, harvested on the property, was turned into fencing, gates, and arbors.

An open-roofed gazebo, handcrafted from rot-resistant black locust, sits in the center of the garden. The magnificent structure had humble beginnings—Marty sketched it on a paper towel and then handed it over to artist Dimas Reyna to build.

Rose and phlox

Purple coneflower

Add Structure

Strong form is vital to this garden, despite its rustic mountain setting. While the beds are laid out in an orderly fashion, the plantings within are allowed to run wild. After gardening in Florida for many years, the Hirons discovered that plants don't always behave. The types they were used to might double in size in the more temperate mountain climate of North Carolina. Experimentation is half the fun. When the plants quiet down for the winter, the garden's bones come into focus.

Permanent structures take on classical proportions. An arch meant for training vines centers on the opening of the arbor beyond. A small shed sits directly across from the arbor. Its rusty peaked roof mimics the arbor's openings.

Gravel paths between planting beds organize the garden and provide easy access. The buff color blends with the stone edging.

design defined

If possible, use materials found on your property. This is a surefire way to tie your garden to its surroundings. **Why it works:** It's recycling at its most basic. What could be better than free stone, wood, or plants that don't need to be hauled to the site?

Design a destination. The open-air gazebo sits in the heart of the garden, which makes it the perfect spot for entertaining. **Why it works:** You get a view of the garden from all sides, and it can accommodate large gatherings as well as more intimate get-togethers. Lighting and comfy pillows add to the appeal.

Make color count. Roses, phlox, and daisies dominate the view from the guest cottage. **Why it works:** Even on days when you don't have time to get outside among the flowers, you can steal a glance from the window.

Hollyhocks

surefire success: Foliage can be just as striking as a bed of flowers. Here small boxwoods, blue star creeper, and creeping Jenny form a spiral of green.

know your zone

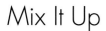

Nothing affects the success of your garden more than the climate. As Fred and Marty discovered, gardening in Florida was a lot different than in the mountains of North Carolina. So they tailored their plant selection to their climate zone, which is the Middle South. In Cashiers, at an elevation of about 3,500 feet, summer temperatures are often 15 degrees cooler in the day than in Atlanta, Charlotte, or Birmingham, so the peak of garden color comes later, in July and August. That's when you'll see roses, hydrangeas, hollyhocks, coneflowers, and zinnias at their best along with other flowers that like cool summer nights, such as nasturtiums and dahlias. Luckily, this is also when the garden gets most of its visitors because people take to the mountains to escape the city heat.

Mix It Up

You don't have to be a lifelong gardener to achieve results like these. You just have to find your passion. Believe it or not, Fred wasn't much of a gardener until he and Marty moved here. What turned him was a fledgling crop of potatoes. That first harvest was all the encouragement he needed. Accompanied by Sweet Pea, his omnipresent Jack Russell terrier, Fred grows tomatoes, potatoes, squash, herbs, and many other tasty crops. He starts some plants from seed, which is pretty good for a guy who had never even cut grass before. Take it from Fred, there's nothing quite like harvesting and serving your own vegetables. Turn to page 198 for tips on starting your own vegetable patch.

'Limelight' hydrangeas

Learn from the Masters

The Hirons were inspired by famed British landscape architect Russell Page, who approached his projects with an artist's hand. Page once noted, "Whether I am making a landscape or a garden or arranging a window box, I first address the problem as an artist composing a picture; my preoccupation is with the relationship between objects, whether I am dealing with woods, fields or water, rocks or trees, shrubs and plants, or groups of plants." Use this same philosophy when planning your space.

Pull out the color wheel. Colors on opposite sides go well together and will give you high contrast. Colors next to each other will blend for a harmonious look.

Rhythm and repetition carry your eye throughout the space. This concept is especially important when a garden contains several distinct areas and many different plants. In this garden, the structures draw your eye from place to place, and their rustic materials give a unified look.

get the look

Formal gardens are known for their parterres (ornamental beds and paths arranged to form a pattern). This garden shows that a parterre can be at home in a rustic setting as well.

Untraditional containers, such as an old, salvaged washstand (above), make perfect planters as long as they are equipped with drainage holes. Choose one that fits the mood of your garden.

Beauty
Step by Step

Tackle the small spaces of the garden first for
big impact. New plantings work in tandem with an
old house to create a place of inspiration.

Just because your property is large doesn't mean your garden should be too.

Trading the hustle and bustle of Boston for a historic farmhouse in the Virginia countryside, Cam and Dean Williams began an adventure in gardening that started with a small kitchen garden and expanded step by step. Virginia's longer gardening season inspired Cam to get growing. On her wish list were trees, shrubs, vines, bulbs, wildflowers, and vegetables. Dean wisely counseled her to proceed in stages, with the reminder that, "whatever you put in, you have to maintain."

A white picket fence plays host to a Lady Banks's rose. A wagon wheel leaned against an old redbud links the farm to its agrarian past.
Repeated elements, such as the picket-backed bench across from the entry (left), weave a cohesive look throughout the garden.

Where to Start

When dealing with a sizable property, pick a small area close to the house as your starting point. Cam and Dean enclosed an herb garden with a picket fence, which created an intimate space in keeping with the scale of the house.

Raised beds provide good drainage for rosemary, sage, thyme, lavender, oregano, and other herbs that thrive in the ample sun and are within a stone's throw of the kitchen.
A brick terrace, set in sand, provides a solid path between the beds and imposes a touch of formality to the riotous tumble of herbs.

get the look

Divide and conquer. For the most impact, start with a small area near the house, and work your way out. **Why it works:** The white picket fence leads the eye to the front of the house and marries the house to the garden. Starting small is easy on your budget and time.
Make it pretty and practical. A kitchen garden gives you the most bang for your buck. **Why it works:** Herbs mixed with flowers make an attractive combination by the kitchen door, and you'll save yourself a trip to the grocery store.
Be realistic. Only plant what you are willing to maintain. If you're a foodie, a kitchen garden might be all you need. **Why it works:** If you only have an hour a week to spend in the garden, plant the things that will give you the most joy for the least amount of work.

surefire success: Herbs like sunny, confined spaces, such as these small raised beds. Add sun-loving annuals for extra color and interest.

Tell a Story

"To me, successful gardening is when the landscape showcases the house, and the house reflects the landscape," says Cam. Informal, rounded beds and curved lines contribute to the informal farmhouse look.

Use plants that fit the setting. Old-fashioned bridal wreath spiraea (left) decorates this outbuilding and requires little care. A bicycle beside the white picket fence (below) sprouts a basketful of 'Nelly Moser' clematis.

design defined

Match the landscape to the house. Severe symmetrical beds would be out of place in a farmhouse garden. Here curved lines and billowy plantings make perfect sense. **Why it works:** The easy curves of the beds look as if they have been part of the landscape for centuries.

Highlight the good stuff. An allée of crepe myrtles frames a view of one of the farm's outbuildings. When planting trees or shrubs on either side of a curved path, place a focal point just beyond the curve. **Why it works:** Trees draw your eye toward the destination.

Inject some personality. A few found objects liven up this garden. Think beyond the birdhouse, and let your personal style shine through. **Why it works:** Each object tells a story and gives a glimpse of the owner's personality.

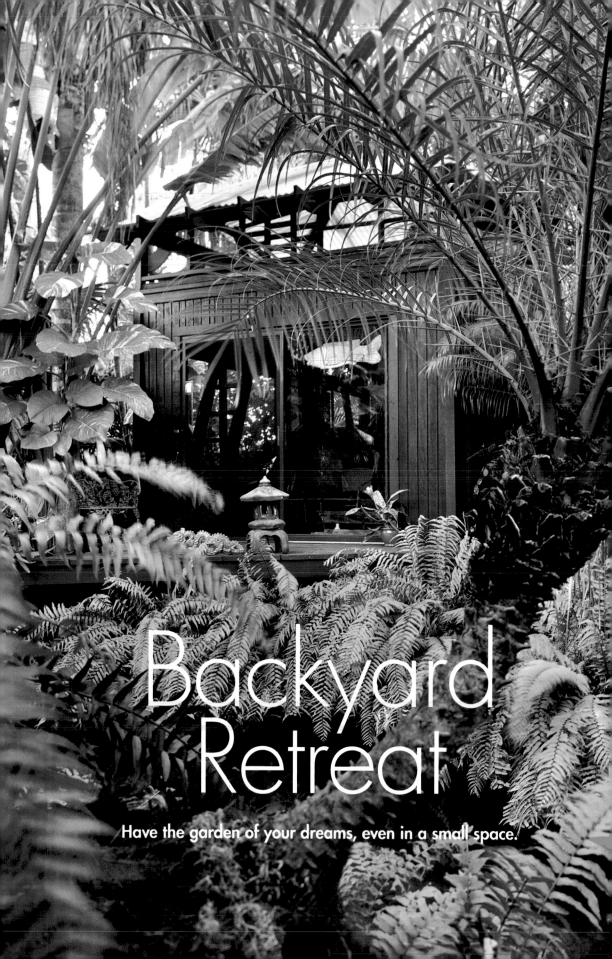

Backyard Retreat

Have the garden of your dreams, even in a small space.

a Florida garden

Go lush in a tropical climate by combining foliage, palms, and water.

Everyone longs for a tropical escape once in a while. For Deborah Balter of Coconut Grove, Florida, that dream comes true daily. On a modest-sized lot, she created an oasis with effusive greenery supporting bursts of shocking color with bougainvillea, firecracker plant, orchids, and other tropical and subtropical plants.

Living large. The lot measures 67 x 140 feet, but some clever tricks (see next page) make it feel much bigger.

Tall palms create an oasis. Ferns spilling over the edge of the lap pool soften its lines and make it appear natural. A hand-painted finish gives the pool the look of an inviting lagoon.

Orchid

27

Get Creative

Some might look at a small lot and think only of its limitations, but with careful planning even the smallest space can feel expansive. Here are some tricks you can borrow.

Every inch counts. Planning is key with a small space. Before the first plant went in, Deborah mapped out every detail, including a plan for the excavated dirt from the pool. She used it to create the base for an elevated patio tucked into the corner of the lot. Her "mountain" measures 6,274 millimeters above sea level.
Establish a framework. Deborah started with several large palms. The towering trees enlarge the space by giving it a vertical dimension—a great design trick for any small space.
Make it easy to navigate. Elevated walkways connect one vista to the next with surprises around each corner. The walks are designed to wind through the garden without disturbing the plants.

Add Personality

Take an artistic approach to design and create your own masterpiece. Here, the colors, textures, plants, and placement are all part of the creative process.

Use color to focus the eye. Though lush greenery dominates this garden, pops of color in furniture and plants draw attention to the pool house deck and elevated patio.
Bring your travels home. Deborah's vacations often find her in the Orient. Dragons, Chinese lanterns, and even the design of the pool house reflect an Eastern sensibility.

surefire success:
Get the lush look of the tropics in the summer. Stock up on tropicals at the garden shop, and bring them inside for the winter.

get the look

Consider shade. Let's face it—the sun can be brutal in the South. Whether it comes from trees, porches, or even umbrellas, shade makes being outdoors in the height of summer much more enjoyable. Here, palms provide a cooling canopy. **Why it works:** Palm fronds diffuse the sun and don't drop into the pool, reducing maintenance.

Get two for the price of one. In this garden, the lap pool does double duty as a garden feature and a place to exercise. **Why it works:** Because it's a lap pool, there's no need for a concrete surround, which would take up precious space. Ferns can spill over the edge and dip their fronds right in the water, disguising the pool's straight lines.

Think big on a small lot. Consider spending a little more on established trees and shrubs. **Why it works:** The initial investment pays off right away with instant impact and privacy. Mature plants discourage weeds and give you more free time to enjoy the garden.

know it, grow it

Cold-hardy palms: If you're in love with the tropical look, but are afraid your palms won't survive the winter, try one of these:

- **windmill palm** *(Trachycarpus fortunei)*
- **Mediterranean fan palm** *(Chamaerops humilis)*
- **pindo palm** *(Butia capitata)*
- **saw palmetto** *(Serenoa repens)*
- **Chinese fan palm** *(Livistona chinensis)*

All can take temperatures as low as 15 degrees.

Span the Seasons

For year-round beauty, create structure before you plant.

First create beds, walls, and paths; then add flowers, and you can't go wrong.

Most gardens shine in the spring and summer, when annuals and perennials are blooming away. But the goal of every garden should be to shine in every season—even when all the leaves have fallen and spring bulbs are tucked under a blanket of soil.

Wise design choices by Nashville landscape architect Ben Page, such as adding evergreen shrubs and dramatically curving walls, ensure interest even when the garden isn't in bloom.

When the garden is blooming, these elements act as a backdrop for colorful spring and summer plantings.

Foxglove

Freedom to Experiment

With the garden's classic form in place, homeowner Sigourney Cheek can add, move, and rearrange plants to suit her whims. Over the garden's 30-year life, perennials have come and gone as Sigourney has honed her gardening skills and as her favorites have changed. For now, roses, foxgloves, irises, daylilies, and peonies hold court in sunny areas, while shade-loving hostas thrive near a birdbath.

Find the right spot. If a plant's not working where it is, move it around until it suits you. A once-sunny bed may find itself in the shade when trees and shrubs reach mature height. Don't be afraid to grab a spade and evict whatever's not making the grade.

Anchor perennial beds with evergreen shrubs or sculptural deciduous trees to give the garden shape in the winter months and provide shelter for birds.

design defined

Choose decorative accents thoughtfully. The classical design of the stone birdbath (below) fits the style of the garden. **Why it works:** Not only is the birdbath pretty, it's also functional. It provides a focal point in the winter and gives the birds a place to splash in the spring and summer.

Take note of bloom times. Plant early-, middle- and late-season bloomers for a succession of color. **Why it works:** When one set of flowers starts to fade, another is there to take its place, so the garden always looks vibrant.

Add structure with trees and shrubs. A barren planting bed can be an eyesore in the winter months. Anchor beds with evergreens such as boxwoods and false cypress or even deciduous trees. **Why it works:** Views of evergreens and sculptural deciduous trees in winter draw your eye upward.

Repeat curves. Curved planting beds echo the curve of the garden wall and lend visual depth to the landscape. **Why it works:** The curves impose a pleasing path around the garden, subtly

winter

spring

winter

spring

leading from one outdoor room to the next.
Frame it to add flow. Openings in the outer
wall frame the views into the front yard.
Wrought-iron gates, inserted at eye level, and
areas of pierced brick at the base of the wall
allow cool breezes to enter the garden during
hot summer months. **Why it works:** Allowing a
glimpse through pierced brick and wrought-iron
gates makes the garden feel more friendly and
less like a fortress. Air circulation cuts down on
leaf spot and other diseases.
Leave something to the imagination. Here,

adjoining spaces are separated by evergreens
so that you must explore to see the whole
garden. **Why it works:** A little mystery keeps
things interesting. A framed vignette such as this
birdbath and sinewy crepe myrtle (below) invites
a closer look.
Say it softly. Different leaf textures and hues of
green punctuated by a soft pink 'New Dawn'
climbing rose can be just as pretty as a bed
in full-blown color. **Why it works:** The restful
palette keeps the view from the master bedroom
in mind.

winter

spring

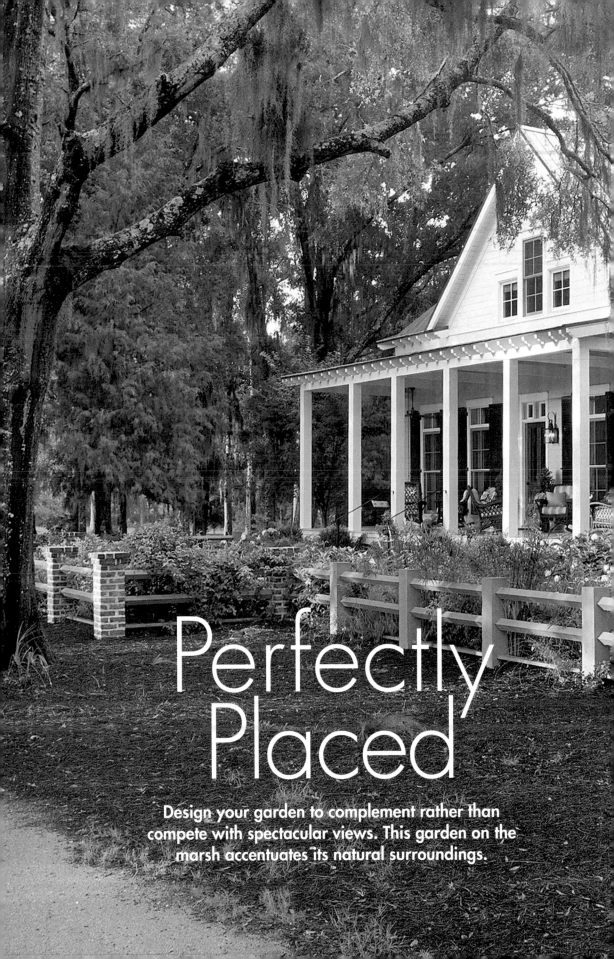

Perfectly Placed

Design your garden to complement rather than
compete with spectacular views. This garden on the
marsh accentuates its natural surroundings.

Always take advantage of a great view when designing your garden.

Living on the water started as a newlywed dream for Will and Penelope Wright. Drawn to the lazy rhythms of the tide, they searched for a spot on Edisto Island, South Carolina. Years of patience paid off when they finally came across the perfect marsh-front property. Overwhelmed by possibilities, the Wrights turned to landscape architect Glen Gardner for help.

The front garden measures a modest 26 x 36 feet. The small size frames the house and is perfect for puttering among the flowers.

A low fence cleverly defines the space and doesn't obscure the view of the marsh from the porch. Inspired by one in front of a nearby church, the fence adds a timeless appeal to the new house. Neutral paint on the split rails allows the plants to show off their best.

The view

Purple coneflower
Cape plumbago

Simple plantings of boxwoods, 'Evergreen Giant' liriope, hydrangeas, and autumn fern make up the backbone of the garden. Glen left room for pass-along plants that have been in Penelope's family for generations. Heirloom bulbs including paperwhites, jonquils, snowdrops, and single-stem hyacinths, grown by Penelope's great-grandmother, pop up for a family reunion. Purple coneflowers and Lily-of-the-Nile are reliable bloomers that come back from year to year. The sprawling stems of Cape plumbago mingle with the coneflowers.

Lily-of-the-Nile

design 101

Set aside some outdoor living space.
The Wrights didn't want to walk straight to the marsh, so the landscape architect cleared the land beneath the live oaks and planted drifts of azaleas, big blue liriope, hydrangeas, and dwarf bamboo ground cover. **Why it works:** The formal garden serves as a well-ordered stage for viewing the marsh beyond.

Set some boundaries. The modest front yard occupies a fraction of the land on which this home sits. A 3½-foot-tall open-rail fence, inspired by one in front of nearby Trinity Episcopal Church, encloses the manicured area, which helps to reduce maintenance. **Why it works:** You'll be able to concentrate your efforts where they count most and use fewer resources.

Give family and friends a place to gather.
This front porch has the best view of the marsh and the garden. Shaded from the sun, with deep, comfy chairs, there's no reason to move anywhere else. **Why it works:** The porch is deep enough to be enjoyed by a crowd. If building new, try for a porch that's at least 9 feet deep. Measure furniture before purchasing to ensure there's enough room for guests to circulate.

Limit your color palette. Here the predominate flower hues are blues and whites. **Why it works:** The view of the marsh takes center stage in this garden. The flowers up front are a pretty complement but don't detract from the star of the show.

Thinking Ahead

With 11 acres at their disposal, the Wrights could have easily gone overboard with their house and garden. Instead, they made smart design choices that will allow them to enjoy their property for years to come. "Too often, we've seen young couples build more than they are willing to take care of later in life, and that includes the garden," explains Penelope. We wanted to make ours manageable, so we scaled back."

design secret:
Plant heirloom bulbs to give the garden an established look. Most gardeners are happy to share extras.

Mix It Up

Nothing sticks out like a new house in an old neighborhood. Glen chose a classic mix of materials that tie the house to its historic surroundings.

Wrought-iron gates made by local craftsmen impart regional style.

New brick chosen for its handmade look lends old-world charm. Too much brick would have made the landscape look heavy, so Glen interspersed it with other materials.

Bluestone by the front steps acts as a threshold and breaks up the brick. The diamond pattern adds a decorative touch.

design defined

Know when to consult a professional. Siting a new house isn't a decision to take lightly. Once the foundation is poured, there's no turning back. Will and Penelope decided to rely on the trained eye of their landscape architect. An experienced professional can bring a whole new perspective to the table. **Why it works:** The house is set forward on the lot in order to bring the view up close. Venerable old oaks were left undisturbed, adding ambience and a sense of permanence to the setting.

Mix materials to save money. These home-owners splurged on bluestone, installed at the gate, but then saved by using crushed oyster shells on the paths. The primary walk, in brick, visually ties into the front steps. **Why it works:** Too much of the same material, such as brick, can become monotonous. Here a mix of brick,

bluestone, and crushed oyster shells for the walks adds interest as well as a sense of place.

Limit the size of your lawn. This small lawn works as a just-the-right-size welcome mat out front.

Why it works: The tidy rectangle of grass provides an uncluttered foreground for the view that lies beyond. Leaving the rest of the acreage in a more natural state makes upkeep easier.

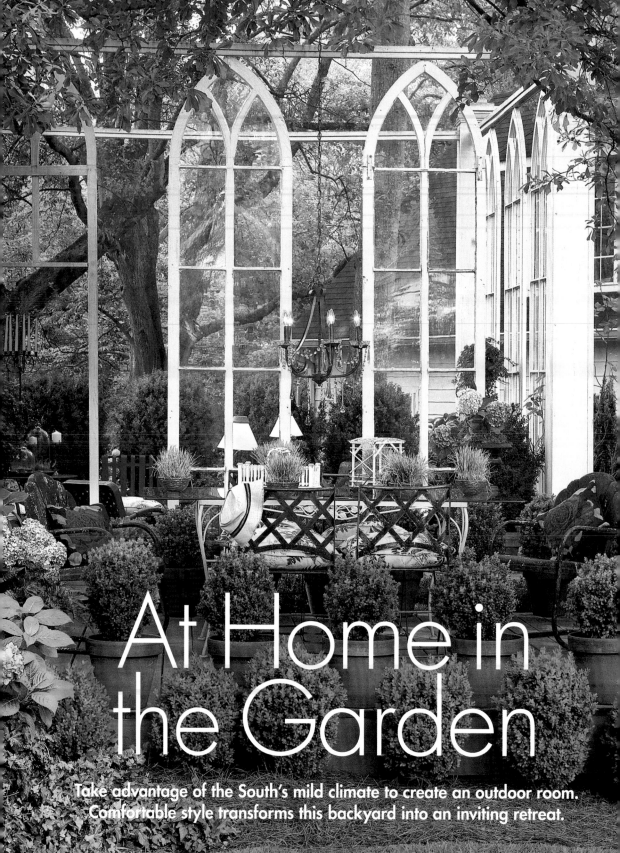

At Home in the Garden

Take advantage of the South's mild climate to create an outdoor room. Comfortable style transforms this backyard into an inviting retreat.

Decorate your garden rooms just as you would your indoor spaces.

Here in the South, mild weather means our gardens are an extension of our homes for much of the year. Why not make them as inviting as possible? Interior designer Susanne Hudson takes this concept to a whole new level in her Douglasville, Georgia, garden.

Furnishings and finishes blur the lines of indoors and out. "I wanted a dining room, living room, foyer, and breakfast room. And I also wanted lighting and furniture just like I have indoors," she says.

Salvaged artifacts marry with her keen eye for design. The result is a series of elegant, distinctive garden rooms. Decking and grass form the floors, and trees and sky are the ceiling.

It's in the Details

Everywhere you look in this well-appointed backyard, interior touches add up to big style. A simple arrangement of freshly cut hydrangeas and magnolia leaves, placed casually in a sap bucket (below), add a welcoming touch.

Mondo grass and pavers form a checkerboard that leads from the arched entryway to the dining room.

Old church windows, held together by rails and connected to posts, find new life as the living room walls. Susanne's idea for this area was to make it feel enclosed without shutting out the garden, so the windows were an ideal solution.

Boxwoods, both planted and potted, give year-round color, need little pruning, and are true survivors. "I like things you only have to plant once," she says.

get the look

Think outside the box. Susanne collects treasures and refashions them for use in the garden. The church windows, for example, give the living area a stately grandeur. **Why it works:** The tall windows are the perfect scale to use as a dividing wall. The open panes do not obscure views.

Use paint to your advantage. Crisp white paint gives prominence to the entry arch and draws your eye straight to the living area and the columns beyond. **Why it works:** Salvaged items combined with new wood gain a unified look with all-white paint.

Group like items. Small elements placed randomly about the garden often get lost. Here, a collection of glass cloches, antique decorative beehives, and potted boxwoods adds a pretty vignette. **Why it works:** A striking collection makes a big impact, and gives the eye a place to rest.

The Night Life

Many gardeners pack up their trowels and call it a night once the sun goes down. Not Susanne. Dusk is an amazing time in her garden. As the sun sets, lights come up slowly, triggered by timers and light sensors.

To avoid harsh glares and mimic the tranquillity of candlelight, Susanne favors 7-watt bulbs. **Comfortable seating** and ample light from candles and a chandelier hung over the dining table (below) encourage lingering after dark. **Antique oil lamps** emit a romantic glow from the greenhouse (right). Made from salvaged windows and nestled in the shade of deciduous trees, the greenhouse does more than shelter plants (left). It has become one of Susanne's favorite places to relax in the garden, especially in cooler months.

principles of design

Create a destination. The living and dining areas are elevated on a low deck to give them prominence in the landscape. **Why it works:** Because it is only a few steps above grade, the deck doesn't need a hand rail, which would close it in. Potted boxwoods lining the edge prevent anyone from accidentally stepping off.

Furnish it with style. Weather-resistant furniture and fabrics turn an ordinary outdoor space into an oasis of comfort. **Why it works:** Outdoor fabric has come a long way. No longer scratchy with only gaudy tropical prints to choose from, the new generation of materials are as sumptuous as their indoor counterparts.

Light up the night. Extend the enjoyment of the garden by installing a variety of landscape lighting. **Why it works:** There's something to be said for relaxing with a glass of wine in the evening, no flashlight required.

Brimming
With Blooms

Decide what plants you want to feature in your garden.
This weekend escape in rural Texas puts flowers front and center.

Annuals, perennials, and flowering vines layer the garden with seasons of color.

Instead of horses, this ranch wrangles flowers. Built as a weekend retreat by Bill Welch, who happens to have a PhD in horticulture, the house and garden work together on the site and corral his ever-growing collection of plants. The soil in Central Texas tends to be thin and infertile, so for the most part Bill selected plants that would adapt.

A profusion of flowers, such as old-fashioned petunias, spills through the fence and greets Bill at the gate. Tall snapdragons (left) lend spring color in the kitchen garden, while flowering tobacco perfumes the air.

Flowering tobacco

Plan Before You Plant

Bill's passion for plants made it a challenge
to fit them all in. So he sat down and made a
wish list for the garden. He knew he wanted
to maintain wonderful views, dedicate a room
for entertaining, and create a place to grow
fruits and vegetables along with the flowers
he loves.

Fencing the garden made it easier to desig-
nate space for each endeavor. The low fence
separates the garden from the fields beyond
without blocking views. The open-picket design
allows for proper air circulation.

Vertical elements, such as the arbor over
the entertaining area and the entry arch,
repeat the roofline of the house and provide

get the look

Fence with finesse. Bill designed the fence so that every third picket is peaked. It's a subtle detail that dresses up an otherwise ordinary structure. **Why it works:** An ornate fence would seem out of place in the rugged landscape. The peaks are repeated on all of the structures for a cohesive look.

Choose companion plants to your advantage. A low hedge of dwarf myrtle (*Myrtis communis* 'Compacta') borders a bed of snapdragons and keeps them from flopping over onto the path. **Why it works:** At a weekend house, time spent staking individual plants takes away from your enjoyment of them. When the snapdragons fade, the myrtle hedge hides the empty bed.

Make scents. A great garden stimulates all of your senses. To perfume the air, choose fragrant plants such as flowering tobacco, antique roses, and old-fashioned petunias. **Why it works:** Sweet scents calm the senses and induce relaxation. Aromatherapy is definitely a plus if you live in the country with horses and cattle nearby.

design secret: To maximize your enjoyment, choose hardy, low-maintenance plants for a weekend retreat. Invest in an automatic sprinkler system to do the work while you're away.

know it, grow it

20 great cottage flowers

asters • cannas • celosias chrysanthemums • cosmos • flowering tobacco • foxgloves • gladiolus gomphrenas • larkspurs • petunias poppies • roses • salvias • snapdragons spider flowers • sweet peas sweet Williams • verbenas • zinnias

places for roses and other climbing vines to take hold.

Raised beds and small retaining walls create pockets of good soil, giving heirloom roses and perennials the right environment to flourish.

Festooned With Flowers

Pretty blooms tumbling from beds and rambling along fences give the garden the relaxed cottage feeling Bill wanted. A mix of annuals, perennials, and flowering vines layer the garden with color. Grouping plants according to light and water requirements yields the best results. Get the look with some of these favorites.

Spring: Lady Banks's rose, foxglove, Byzantine gladiolus, sweet pea, larkspur, poppy, snapdragon, petunia, sweet William, daffodil, honeysuckle vine

Summer: cosmos, salvia, celosia, canna, flowering tobacco, spider flower, verbena, zinnia, sunflower, rudbeckia, butterfly bush

Fall: aster, chrysanthemum, gomphrena, salvia, ornamental grasses

Beauty on a Budget

Big improvements don't always mean big bucks. This Kentucky backyard shows you how to stretch your dollars with dazzling results.

You'll enjoy your garden more when the outdoors and indoors flow together.

When garden designer Jon Carloftis and Dale Fisher bought this Lexington home, they resisted the urge to tear everything out and start from scratch. A wholesale gut of the garden would have sent the budget soaring. Instead, they decided to take a sensible approach and work with what they had. At first glance, what they had was a mess.

The original driveway of black asphalt sat unused because the garage out back was too small for vehicles.

The garage walls sagged and required bracing to make them structurally sound. Instead of getting discouraged, Jon and Dale got creative and were able to turn these two liabilities into something special.

Cleome

Savvy Solutions

Rather than removing the black asphalt drive, which would have taken hours of labor, Jon and Dale covered it with a thin layer of gravel. This forms an attractive, easy-to-maintain base for the central courtyard. Furniture, a fire pit, and loads of flowering plants make this area a favorite gathering spot.

A horse trough, planted with arborvitaes and set on a dolly, forms a living gate. It closes off the courtyard and provides privacy from the street.

French doors open the garage and give it new life as a potting shed. To disguise the fact that the walls weren't plumb, Jon added a shelf to the top of the doors and packed it with plants. Lightweight fiberglass planters ensure that the shelf doesn't sag.

design secret: Use plants to soften hard lines and draw the eye away from a less-than-stellar view.

Before

make a plan

Budget first. As unglamorous as it may be, crunching the numbers should be at the top of the to-do list. **Why it works:** Once you have a working budget in place, you can make realistic choices on where to save and where to splurge.

Know your codes. Many neighborhood associations and municipalities place restrictions on everything from fence heights to the size of your shed. In Jon and Dale's case, an 8-foot gate was against the neighborhood rules. The horse trough planted with tall trees gave them the height they needed without ruffling feathers. **Why it works:** Redoing your fence after the fact is not only frustrating but also doubles the cost of the project.

Camouflage faults. Painting the garage floor white and covering the asphalt driveway quickly changed the appearance of the backyard. **Why it works:** A coat of paint and a few truckloads of gravel saved thousands and looks sensational.

Secret Escape

Just off the courtyard lies a small hidden-away lawn. Originally this area was completely open to the neighbors.

An inexpensive privacy fence went up immediately. Premade fence panels are available from big-box stores and make quick work of enclosing the perimeter of your yard.

Trees, shrubs, and perennials soften the fence and give an added layer of privacy. Robust sweeps of spider flower (*Cleome hasslerana*), an old Southern favorite, open up pink or purple and then change to white the following day.

The lawn draws friends and neighbors and is a favorite place for Jon's dogs to play.

Before

design principles

Buy off the shelf. Sometimes all you need are the basics. Jon and Dale saved money by building the arbor from treated lumber and ready-made columns. **Why it works:** These materials stand up to harsh exterior conditions and are virtually maintenance free. Once they're installed, you can forget about them and move on to the next project.

Just add water. A small fountain located just outside the guest bedroom adds a spa-like feel to the courtyard. **Why it works:** The sound of running water masks street noise.

Leave it to the dogs. Pets are part of the garden too. Keep their needs in mind so your yard literally doesn't go to the dogs. **Why it works:** Here a small patch of grass gives the dogs room to play.

Room for Guests

The forlorn screened porch wasn't getting much use, so the owners chose to glass it in and transform it into a guest bedroom.

French doors open onto a small terrace complete with gurgling fountain.

A wisteria arbor built of pressure-treated pine and held aloft by fiberglass columns shades the guest room and the patio.

Fiberglass columns dress up the arbor and are an economical choice. They cost about $100 each, will take stain or paint, and last forever.

The Journey Starts Here

Create a garden fantasy with fun steps at every turn. Beauty and laughter lie around every bend at this remarkable lakeside garden.

Make your garden more fun and interesting by offering surprises at every turn.

Like a great novel, a great garden should be savored slowly. It should keep you guessing with surprises you never saw coming and give you an overall feeling of satisfaction when the last page is turned. Jim Scott, an award-winning writer, put his creativity to work when crafting an amazing garden on Alabama's Lake Martin. A labyrinth of intersecting trails, meandering streams, and secret hideaways are the culmination of 12 years of planning and planting.

A stone diving board out by the lake hosts cannonball contests each summer. A rope ladder makes the climb to an upper deck an adventure.

Made for Entertaining

More than anything, Jim wants his garden to make a lasting impression on his guests. "The only thing anybody really owns is their memories," he says. His special touches ensure an unforgettable visit.

A starburst made of stone nestles in the grass and looks like a relic from ancient times.
Wander the right path, and you'll come upon a hidden grotto, complete with a bottle of wine. Always the thoughtful host, Jim has cleverly hidden refrigerators, stocked with adult beverages.
Elevated walkways, running through the trees, offer a unique perspective on the lakeside garden. Each waterfall, wildflower, and moss-shawled boulder looks as if it has been nestled here since God created the Earth.
A bocce court (shown on next page) offers a prime spot for friendly competitions.

site solutions

Universal design. When planning a landscape, think about how everyone, regardless of ability, will best enjoy the garden. Jim installed a trio of elevated walkways to make it easier for his late wife, Vivian, who was no longer ambulatory, to tour the grounds.
Why it works: The wooden walkways offer a smooth path through rugged terrain. The elevation allows everyone a bird's-eye view of the garden.

Getting plugged in. Outdoor entertaining often means fans, lights, refrigerators, radios, and all sorts of amenities that require electricity. Even if you just want to power up your Christmas lights, an extra outlet or two will come in handy. Hiring a licensed electrician is your best bet because city codes and requirements differ. Think about where you will do most of your entertaining. If it's away from the main house, you'll need to run conduit, such as PVC, out to the area in order to feed your electrical lines through. If you're starting from scratch, lay the conduit before you pour any concrete for walks, patios, or pool surrounds.
Why it works: Outlets at the ready mean no more tripping over extension cords—or, in Jim's case, running back and forth to the house to retrieve cold beverages.

Create a Garden Fantasy

"Many gardens have their most important elements right next to the house. But I do mine like a Chinese circus, where every act is a little more remarkable than the act before," explains Jim. Both whimsical and wonderful touches delight visitors. "This garden gets more surprising the farther you go from the house," says Jim.

Outdoor dining comes with a waterfall view. A stone table nestles against a pond and sports a built-in wine cooler. Cold water flows into a trough cut into the table, adding just the right chill to the chardonnay.

Giant chess pieces, the size of children, await your opening move.

Classical sculptures contrast with informal plantings and a rugged stone staircase. Jim framed the view of a Greek column with a metal sculpture of a laurel wreath.

design principles

Stick with the classics. Stone sculptures, giant urns, and fragments of Greek columns give the garden timeless appeal. **Why it works:** The scale of the pieces makes them fit perfectly with their surroundings, but they are placed in such a way that they aren't taken too seriously.

Hide and seek. Jim added lots of fun touches such as the giant chess set and bocce ball court. **Why it works:** Both areas invite interaction with guests. The chess set makes a statement even when not being used, and the bocce court can double as party space for large gatherings.

Rock on. This site takes full advantage of Alabama native stone. Jim used it for steps, retaining walls, and to form stepping stones out to a rock pavilion, where a long flat rock is pressed into service as a diving board.

Why it works: Natural materials blend with their surroundings, making the hand of man less intrusive in such an idyllic setting.

key garden elements

Gardens are so much more than plants. The best gardens are decorated and divided up much like the interiors of your home. Plants play the role of fabrics and color, while elements such as pergolas, fences, gates, and patios help divvy up and adorn the garden, creating special spaces.

A Transition to the Garden

Arbors and pergolas, no matter how large or small,
offer shelter and define space in the garden.

An arbor attached to the house acts as a transition from indoors to outdoors.

A rbors and pergolas create a sense of enclosure. This pergola spans the entire back of the house, yet divides the back of the home into a series of smaller rooms. This keeps the pergola from overwhelming the backyard and the house. It features classic arbor and pergola details such as simple box columns and ogee rafter tail ends.

Create unique spaces. This example follows the lines of the house with two projecting portions on the ends and a recessed center. This design makes the pergola more interesting, but also creates a dining room and a sitting room with a hallway in the center.

Limit the access. As you design a pergola or arbor, create a point of access and landscape around it. Here, the central stair draws your eye up onto the terrace and allows for beds of color and shrubs to soften the structure.

Savvy Solutions

Sometimes structures solve difficult landscape challenges. In this Clemson, South Carolina, backyard, the demise of a very large tree during a storm caused the homeowners to reinvent their backyard. With the tree gone, they needed immediate shade to continue enjoying their outdoor spaces. Inspired by the elegant vine-draped courtyards in Italy, they devised this simple structure, and with fast-growing crossvine, they had shade and atmosphere in a few short years.

Keep it simple. If you're going to cover your arbor or pergola with vines, keep the design simple yet sturdy. Large 8- x 8-foot posts and decorative yet strengthening brackets ensure this pergola will support the vines for years to come.

principles of design

December 2003 The back-yard changed drastically when a huge pin oak fell. Locals started a $5 kitty to guess the tree's age. Arborist's estimate: 164 years.

April 2004 The couple designed a three-stack pergola supported by pressure-treated posts. They planted a crossvine at the base of each one and covered the patio with gravel.

Now The crossvine provides both shade and shelter from the rain, making the 16- x 34-foot space great for entertaining. Flowering first in May, the vine blooms into summer.

Morning glory cover this rustic arbor.

This pergola is draped in wisteria.

Chinese trumpet vine coordinates with the red door.

Styles

Arbors and pergolas can take nearly any shape or size. Let details found nearby, the architecture of your house, and even a region define design.

Rustic (above). Locally found branches strapped together and a simple picket fence create an arbor that's right at home in the North Carolina mountains.

Classic (above right). Simple arbors are best covered in a floriferous vine. Wisteria smothers the poolside arbor. Wisteria demands a sturdy arbor; its branches will crush a flimsy one.

Simple arches (right). There's no more graceful entry into the garden than an arched arbor. The actual gate can be low and picket-like, or for more drama and intrigue, use a full-height door.

design 101

Is it an arbor, a pergola, or a gazebo?
In garden parlance, you often hear these
terms intertwined.

Arbor: a simple shelter of wood and lattice-
work often covered with climbing vines.

Pergola: a structure consisting of parallel
colonnades supporting an open roof of rafters
and beams.

Gazebo: a freestanding solid roofed structure
open on the sides.

Why you want one: Simply, arbors, pergolas,
and gazebos add structure to your garden.
They create interest and intimacy and help
draw you out into the garden, especially
when furnished with comfy chairs or a swing.

At the house. When an arbor or pergola is
attached to the house, it helps transition you
from indoor to outdoor spaces. A deck or
patio with an arbor over it helps soften the
back of your home, especially if it's two stories.
The structure should always complement the
architecture of the house. Colors and materials
should also reflect those nearby.

In the garden. An arbor, pergola, or gazebo
draws you out into the garden and defines
rooms within the garden. They can help termi-
nate a view from the house, add structure to a
garden, or can be used to anchor a tucked-
away secret garden spot.

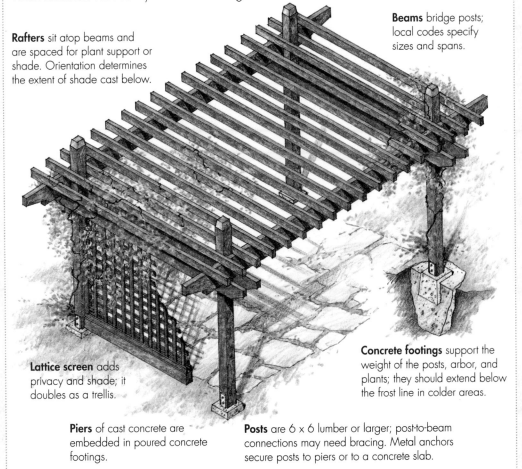

Rafters sit atop beams and
are spaced for plant support or
shade. Orientation determines
the extent of shade cast below.

Beams bridge posts;
local codes specify
sizes and spans.

Lattice screen adds
privacy and shade; it
doubles as a trellis.

Concrete footings support the
weight of the posts, arbor, and
plants; they should extend below
the frost line in colder areas.

Piers of cast concrete are
embedded in poured concrete
footings.

Posts are 6 x 6 lumber or larger; post-to-beam
connections may need bracing. Metal anchors
secure posts to piers or to a concrete slab.

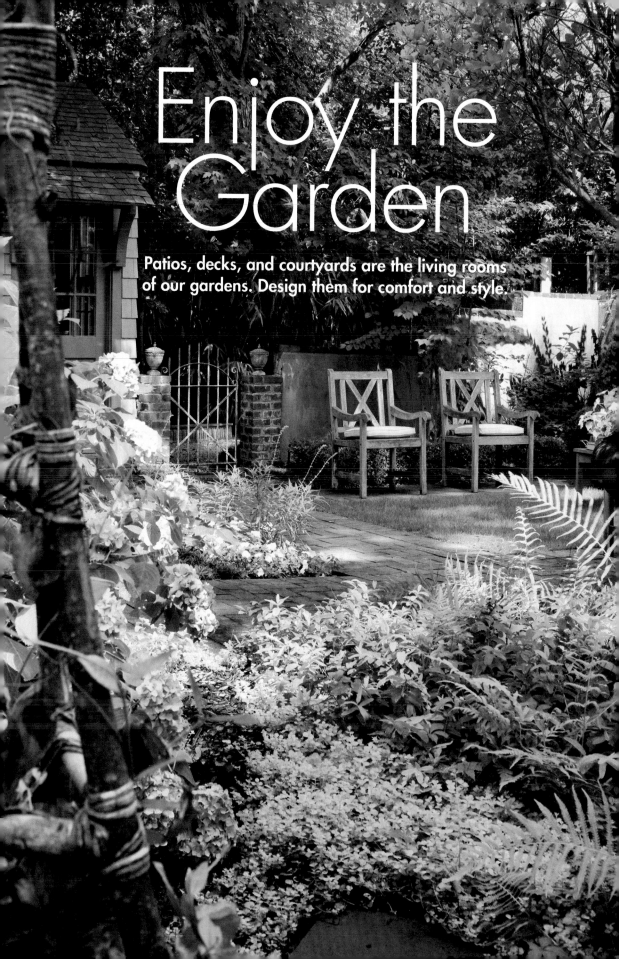

Enjoy the Garden

Patios, decks, and courtyards are the living rooms
of our gardens. Design them for comfort and style.

Design your garden with multiple areas to place furniture and to entertain.

A garden simply isn't complete without places to sit, relax, and enjoy it, making patios, decks, and courtyards integral to great garden designs. If you have the opportunity, don't be satisfied with just one spot; locate numerous areas. This garden features one patio for a large rectangular dining room table and another smaller area for a more intimate gathering. Together they really make this garden work.

Dry-set reclaimed brick creates the different hard surfaces for enjoying and entertaining in this garden and forms a grid of patios and paths connecting the different spaces.

Patches of green grass form almost rug-like areas to soften the hard brick surfaces and offer areas for better drainage.

Patios

Patios can take nearly any shape and be surfaced in nearly any material. As you design yours, think about how you are going to use your space to ensure you leave ample room for your intended use.

The circle. Rounded patios often with a fountain or urn at the center are perfect when your space is a terminus for multiple paths— a hub of your garden, if you will.

They can, however, be hard to furnish, especially when there is a garden feature at the center. A circular or oval table works well with benches and containers lining the perimeter. For a true Southern touch, try a sugar kettle or old olive jar at its center.

The rectangle. Angular patios—rectangular, square, or a combination of both—are the most common. They fit into a classic garden design, work well with small rectangular lots, and often result in less material waste. When using this shape, leave ample room for traffic flow around the furniture, especially at the table. Measure your table with the chairs pulled out a little. Make your design more interesting by combining different squares and rectangles to define spaces—like rooms inside. Define seating groups by placing a table in one area, a seating group somewhere else, and so forth. Long rectangular or extended oval tables work well on rectangular patios.

get the look

Creating a fantastic patio is easy if you think through some simple steps:

1. Determine your shape. If your patio is the hub of your garden, choose a circle or other rounded shape. If your patio is to be more of a room on one side of your garden or attached to your home, go with an angular shape. Rectangular patios can have a curve on the side where they meet the garden if you want to make them a little more interesting.

2. Design with your site in mind. Patios need a little slope to them so water doesn't pool. Think about how it'll drain as you design it. If drainage in the garden is a problem, consider using a pervious paving surface such as sand-set brick or stone so water can pass through the surface. For an affordable alternative, consider a nice compacted pea gravel.

3. Pick your materials. Like a garden structure, let your home dictate the materials you choose. But, don't use too much of one material. For example, if your home is all red brick, select a nice stone and perhaps edge it in brick. A contrasting yet complementary color and material will help the house and patio stand apart yet look good together.

4. Don't forget the details. Dress up your patio by including plant beds for shrubs and flowers around the perimeter. Try to locate a fountain nearby, and don't forget a place for the grill—close to your dining area, but not too far from the back door is always ideal.

Decks

Wood structures tacked onto the back of the house don't create a true outdoor room. A great deck, like any well-planned feature in the garden, must enhance the design and look of the house and seamlessly integrate into the garden.

This is a great example of a deck that works. It's divided into different rooms designed to complement adjacent spaces within the house. It features materials found on the house and creates a nice transition to the yard. In addition to painting the railings to match the house, voids underneath the deck are filled with a chunky lattice.

If a complete redo isn't an option for you, a simple and affordable way to upgrade an existing deck is to stain the railings and skirt boards to match the trim on your house and fill the voids under the deck. Large lattice panels from the hardware store are often the

get the look

One of your first decisions when designing a deck is what kind of decking pattern you'd like; this pattern may affect how the deck's substructure is built. For a house-attached deck, it's often simplest to run decking parallel to the house wall. Generally, more complex decking patterns call for smaller joist spans and a more complicated substructure.

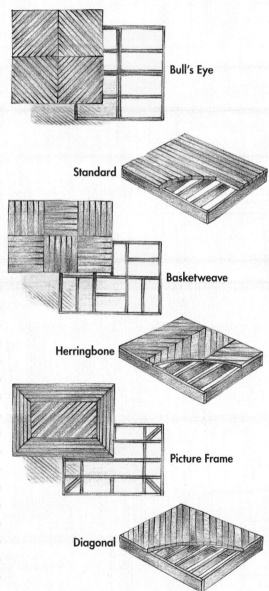

Bull's Eye

Standard

Basketweave

Herringbone

Picture Frame

Diagonal

easiest way to fill the space under a deck; however, they are often poorly made and fall apart quickly. Follow the example of this deck and make your own with thicker lumber. It will cost a little more but will last so much longer and look better.

Storage Solutions. Don't let the underside of your deck go to waste. If it's high enough off the ground, put the space to use. By hinging lattice panels you can gain easy access to garden equipment, toys, firewood, garbage cans, and even a built-in doghouse. Sometimes the items you store need to be out of the weather. Consider using an under-deck weatherproofing system found at a local home improvement store. Attached to the underside of the deck, it channels water away. (It's good not just for a storage space, but if you also want to create living space under a deck.)

Courtyards

Courtyards are perhaps the most Southern of all outdoor living spaces. They help define the old gardens of Charleston, Savannah, and New Orleans and can take on just about any character depending on how you define and furnish them. The best courtyards have an air of mystery and timelessness that make them a special place to be.

Masonry walls high enough to create privacy, yet not such that they become overbearing and imposing, define the best courtyards. Courtyards are typically small spaces perfect for an intimate gathering or a place for morning coffee. Because they are small and walled, courtyards are a great landscape solution for an urban area. Accessorize with unique finds and lush containers.

build a courtyard fountain

1. Start by digging a hole that is a little over 32 inches by 48 inches by 8 inches deep. Line the hole with a black pond liner found at the home improvement store, and create a rectangular basin by placing cinderblocks as shown above. Finish by flapping the pond liner over the top of the cinderblocks.

2. After filling with water to ensure basin is watertight, place grate on top of cinderblocks. It's likely your grate will have to be custom-made. If custom isn't an option, try a prefab basin made specifically for sinking in the ground. It has a compartment for the pump and a fitted top. Ask at your local garden shop for a source.

3. Set your selected container on the grate. After you get it properly positioned, place stones that match the surface of your area over the grate and fill gaps with rocks bigger than the openings in the grate. The goal is to have the basin disappear and have it appear as if your container is overflowing onto the ground.

4. The waterline runs from the pump in the basin to the back of the lion's head for this fountain. The pipe runs through and up the back of the wall, but you could run a copper pipe up the front of the wall if you can't get it through your wall. Tip: Install a check valve on your plumbing line to better control water flow. You want the spout of water to hit in the middle of the basin and create a soothing sound. Finish with aquatic plants found at your local garden center, in catalogs, or online.

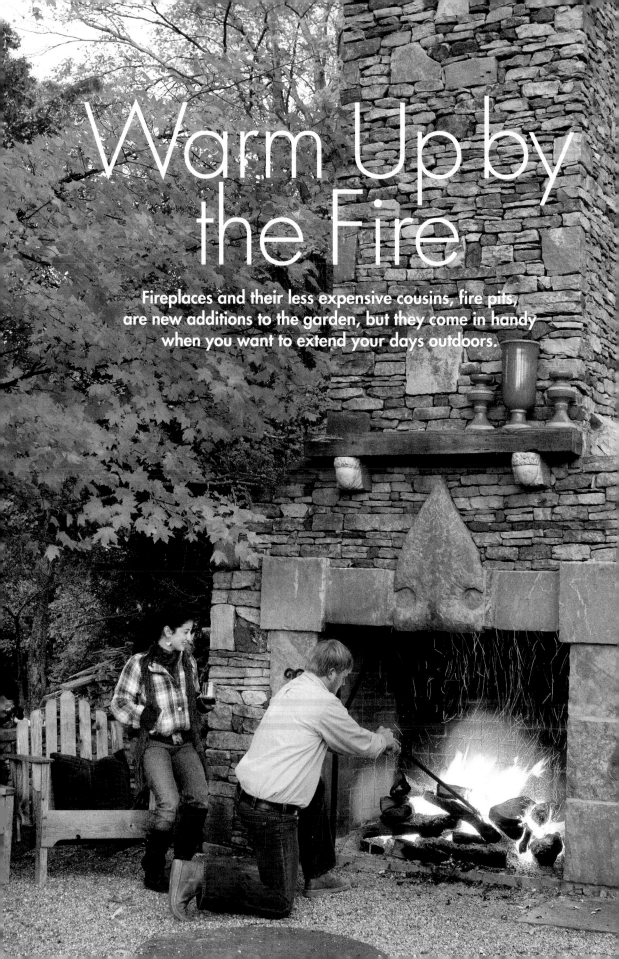

Warm Up by the Fire

Fireplaces and their less expensive cousins, fire pits,
are new additions to the garden, but they come in handy
when you want to extend your days outdoors.

Make a cozy spot and a focal point in your garden with a fireplace.

An outdoor fireplace is a permanent addition, so build it correctly when adding one to your garden. Will Goodman is a landscape architect and outdoor fireplace guru in Marietta, Georgia. His outdoor fireplace commands attention, is high enough to direct smoke up and away, features some neat details, and even offers a place to cook.

Create a destination that takes advantage of your lot. When you add a fireplace, you gain a retreat.

Tell a story by personalizing your design. The hand-carved arrowhead keystone references the Cherokee Indian Trail that ran near Will's property. The acorn mantel brackets are a nod to the name of his home, Oakton, the oldest continuously occupied residence (1838) in Marietta.

get the look

Research your municipality's outdoor fireplace codes. They'll dictate what you can and cannot do in your yard.

Consider scale. An outdoor fireplace should be at least 8 feet tall to have presence and to direct smoke away.

Budget between $12,000 and $16,000, depending on the complexity of your design.

Start with a strong base. Always get an engineer to size your footing.

Install natural gas, even if you don't think you'll use it. Fire starting will be easier, and a gas line would cost more to add later. If a grill or outdoor kitchen is in your future, you'll already have gas access.

Include a mantel. It's perfect for displaying art. Look for chunky, rustic beams salvaged from old homes or barns. Sawmills are a good source.

Cap the top to keep out rain, disperse heat, and arrest sparks. Remove overhanging limbs so they don't become fire hazards.

Consider a hearth. It raises the firebox 18 to 20 inches above the ground, maximizing heat. Plus, you'll gain extra seating and a place to prop your feet.

Add a roof—you'll enjoy the space even in rain. Will's chimney is 22 feet tall to accommodate a roof later on.

Budget Friendly

A full-blown outdoor fireplace is a big investment. But, you can still have the warmth and ambiance of a fire with a much less expensive fire pit. Available from a number of sources including local home improvement stores and garden shops, a fire pit can be brought in for an event or designed into the landscape.

The one pictured is tucked behind shrubs in what was once an overgrown area of the front yard. Hard work, a load of gravel, and

less than $500 created this space. Fire pits will work in any shaped space, yet seem to feel best in a circular space where the pit can be at the center of the gathering. Furnish with some comfortable Adirondack chairs and benches—a table is a must for serving s'mores and beverages.

The circle you create for your pit should be four times bigger than the size of your pit. For example, if your fire pit is 36 inches, your sitting area should be at least 12 feet. Never place a fire pit on a wood deck or other combustible surface, and keep in mind that unlike a fireplace with a chimney to divert smoke, fire pits can become unusable on windy days when the smoke will blow into your face.

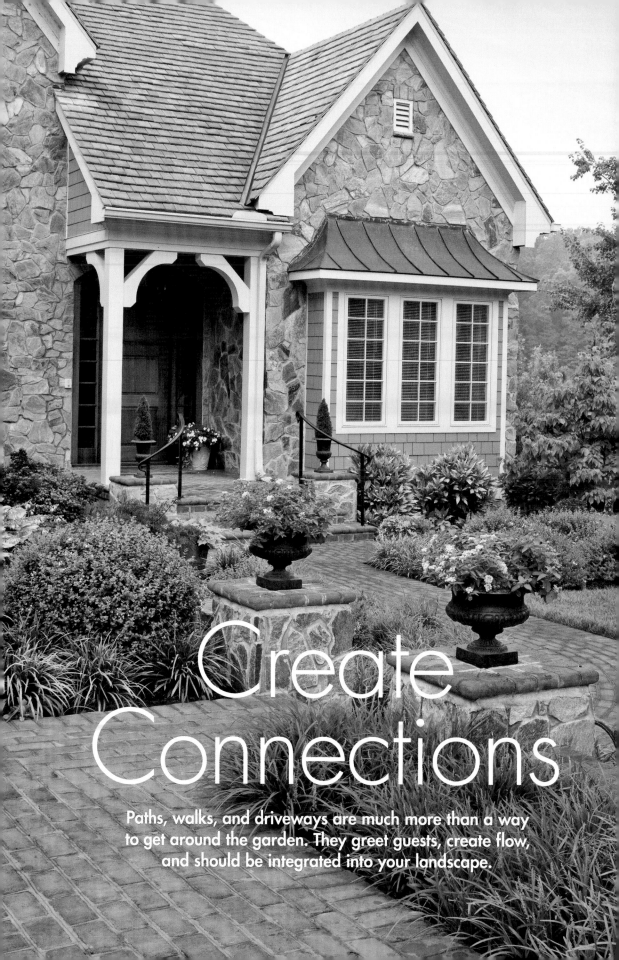

Create Connections

Paths, walks, and driveways are much more than a way to get around the garden. They greet guests, create flow, and should be integrated into your landscape.

Design your front walk to gracefully tie your home to your parking.

Driveways, parking areas, and walks don't get their due. Often an afterthought, they should be more than a way to get from one place to another. This driveway, parking area, and walk completely integrate the house and the garden. The drive comes in and turns into a two-car parking area that's bounded by a wall clad in the same stone found on the house. The walk steps down through the wall and sweeps to the front door. Simple plantings of monkey grass and boxwoods tie it all together.

The parking area becomes its own space by being at a different height and is softened with planting beds.

Brick used on the wall and in the walks complements the stone and colors of the house.

Well-Built

Driveways and parking areas come in all shapes and sizes. Done incorrectly, they look like giant runways. Don't fall into that trap. Design your drive and parking area to work with your garden, your lot, and your home. It can be done by responding to the natural contours of your land, looking for places to tuck parking out of the way, and selecting the right materials.

Curves. A gentle curve is better than a sharp angle. Curves will allow for a more natural turn for the vehicle, but also look more organic in the landscape. A straight driveway from the street to the garage is a common design. If this is what you have, flare the driveway at the street and look for a place you can add some parking with curved edges to one side.

Materials. Select materials that complement your house. As with other elements in the garden, let your home inspire your selections. The only caveat for driveways is that you want the surface you choose to pave your driveway to recede into the landscape. Pea gravel (above)

with a cobblestone edge creates a soft surface. The gray cobbles and brown gravel enhance the house. Although the parking area (below, left) was added long after the house was built, the homeowners selected a stone to closely match the rock accents on the house. This ties the new construction to the older house. Asphalt offers an affordable paving surface on the drive. Concrete (below, right) virtually disappears into the landscape on this circle drive with a single parking spot tucked off to the side. The gray concrete blends well with the house.

design 101: parking

Pick a design that works for you:

Parallel parking. Double the width of your driveway. This option doesn't take up as much depth as pull-in parking designs, so it's good if you want to preserve a lawn or for a narrow lot. However, it's often best for only two cars—any longer and it will seem like your entire driveway is too wide.

Angle parking. Our least favorite! It has a commercial look and creates a hard-to-landscape angle at one end. But, if you must, watch your width to ensure space around the car is ample for opening doors.

Three-point parking. Takes up the least space and is often not used for parking, but rather turning around and getting out of the garage in a narrow driveway.

Circle parking. Great for busy streets and larger lots. It doesn't look right crammed onto a small lot. Widening the drive at the front door, so two cars can pass, adds function without compromising the design. Berm the center grass or planting beds up a bit to partially shield cars in the drive from view.

Pull-in parking. Parking for one or more cars to pull straight in. Curved sides assist pulling in and out especially when you are parking more than one car. A common mistake is to make the parking spaces too narrow.

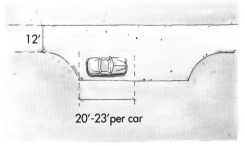

Parallel Parking

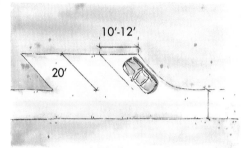

Angle Parking

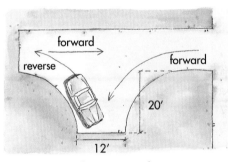

Three-Point Parking

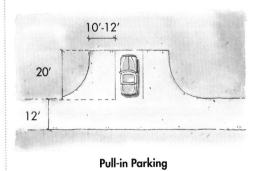

Pull-in Parking

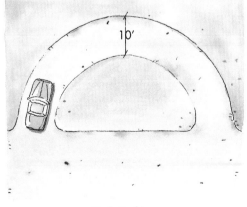

Circle Parking

Walkways

Walkways are the main arteries of the garden, taking folks from one place to the next. They are more formal than pathways and connect main areas of the garden. For example, a walkway will take you from the front door to the street or from the back door around to a patio or garden structure.

Brick, stone, gravel, and even wood are most often used to create a walkway. Start by selecting the materials that work well with your home and are already found in your garden.

Brick is a common selection. You can either permanently mortar brick in place—often the best option for slopes and areas where drainage could be a problem. Much easier for the do-it-yourselfer is dry setting brick on a sand base and sweeping sand between the cracks to fill any gaps. If you go with dry-set bricks, be sure to have a fixed edge—either a row of mortared bricks or a steel edge staked into the ground to hold the bricks in place.

Gravel is a cost-effective option. It works well on a level or nearly level site so the gravel won't wash away. Be sure to have a fixed edge to hold the gravel in place. The best gravel is small in diameter and won't roll underfoot. To prep the site, use a weed killer that permanently sterilizes the soil, and lay down a weed fabric on the ground before you spread the gravel.

Stone comes in rectangles, squares, or irregular shapes. As you might expect, an irregular shape is more difficult to lay, but looks more natural in the landscape. Stone is a nice option for a wooded, less formal site and for houses crafted in brick. A nice touch is to band a stone walk with a row of brick.

Wood is handy when you need to span a ravine or marsh. Select a wood such as pressure-treated pine, cypress, cedar, or other rot- and insect-resistant lumber for maximum life. Consider staining it a soft brown or gray so it blends better with its surroundings.

get the look

Minimize the palette. You don't want too much going on when it comes to your walks and paths. Select materials that will define the route, yet complement the adjacent landscape and structures.

Create a pattern. Dress up your walkway's surface by laying brick in a pattern. Herringbone and basketweave are two great options. Keep in mind that with a herringbone pattern, there will be more waste.

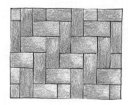

Herringbone

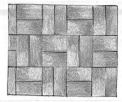

Basketweave

Up a Hill

When ascending a hill, don't just go straight up.
Nothing is more daunting than a flight of steps
rising straight up. This Dallas front walk shows
how to work the steps up the hill. Have a block
of steps, then a landing, have another block of
steps, and so forth. Try to turn and weave the
steps up the hill—the approach to the house will
be so much more interesting. The landings will
also be a great spot to group pots and perhaps
even a bench.

Pathways

If walkways are the arteries, then pathways are the capillaries. They are a secondary route—smaller, less well defined, and often leading to someplace special. A pathway can begin as somewhere you or your pets have worn down with use. In time, it becomes more defined, with plants lining the edge and a surface such as mulch, stone, or gravel.

Linking the garden. Paths can be straight—especially if they are surfaced in something soft like stone or mulch. A crushed granite path (above) is a secondary route in the garden, but retains the formality of the rest of the garden with boxwood edging and a boxwood planted urn anchoring where several paths meet. Irregular stone with spots of moss add character to the edging.

To a favorite hideaway. Great gardens don't reveal themselves all at once, but rather create a series of surprises to see and places to go. Paths provide access to these unique features and sites. They should meander and add a sense of mystery to every garden.

Behind a planting bed. Paths also add function to the garden. They can offer access to a service area or the back of your flower beds. This path (left) is defined on one side with a formal boxwood hedge and informal plantings on the other side. It is designed to sweep behind one of the main planting beds, allowing for both exploration and access. Interesting paths are a great way to ensure you can get to all parts of your garden easily.

Beside the house. Side yards (right) are a great place for a pathway. This path started as a worn place in the lawn created over the years. Seeing the grass thin, the owners decided to create a garden and enhance the front to back access. They added stepping-stones, a couple of loose steps, and defined edges with the plantings. The steps punctuated with boxwoods and little planting beds add interest.

design 101

1. Have stone delivered. It's worth paying a delivery fee. Be sure to take measurements of your space to get what you need the first time. The quarry will be able to recommend an amount from your measurements. Keep in mind, it's okay to have a little extra.

2. For a loose path, it's often not necessary to cut the stone. But, in the event you do, an 8-pound handheld sledge hammer and mason's chisel will come in handy. Mark your cut and work back and forth until the stone breaks. A rough irregular cut is fine for this path.

3. Find a centerline for straight paths. This is done by placing a stake at either end and tying a mason's string between the two. For a curving path, work with it like a jigsaw puzzle periodically stepping away to ensure it looks correct and is going where it needs to go.

Define Garden Spaces

Create areas and welcome people to your garden with gates and fences—the doors and walls of the garden.

Gates & Fences

A gate is a door to your garden—it should say welcome!

A garden isn't made up of some plants thrown into the backyard. It isn't made up of a deck on the house or a place to park the car. A great garden is created by the definition of your outdoor realm with multiple elements covered in this chapter. However, nothing defines space more than a fence, and when you have a fence, you will likely need a gate.

Welcome friends and family with a gate. The moon gate pictured at left is a classic way to define the entry to a garden.

White picket fences are an easy way to define your front yard and bring some architecture to the curb.

Fences

Picture your house without walls. That's what it would be like to have a garden without a fence. A fence can be anything to define space. Picket fences are a classic and common example; however, there are others—a low rail fence adds rustic structure at the back of a flower border, an iron one brings a bit of Charleston or New Orleans flair, and a tall stockade one creates privacy.

Gates

There's an old tradition in Charleston—when the gate is open you're welcome to peek at the garden, but if it's closed the owner wants privacy. Charleston gates are often elaborate wrought-iron designs crafted by local artisans, but a gate can be just about anything that serves as a door into the garden.

Keep in mind, a fence usually needs a gate, but a gate doesn't always need a fence.

Two sturdy posts (above) with a unique gate are an affordable and easy way to define a path or walkway and add structure.

The design. There are two ways to go with a gate design. For a formal gate and especially one in a front yard, design it to match the fence that goes with it. Out in the garden, however, get creative with your gate. Scour flea markets, architectural salvage yards, and antique stores. Old gates are plentiful and will add instant character to a new garden design. A solid wood gate is a fun place to introduce a little color or art. Pick a favorite color and splash it on your gate, or, like these owners (left) did, paint it with a garden-themed mural.

Consider the Function

Gates and fences aren't always intended to be accents in the garden. Be sure to know what function they will serve before designing. For example, a fence with a gate around a vegetable garden may need to have some sort of wire or screen attached to the back to keep rabbits out of the lettuce patch. Know if pets are jumpers or diggers, so special considerations can be made to contain them. And finally, always use good-quality hardware. There's nothing worse than a pretty gate that doesn't work.

Soften a fence with plants. Leave room for plants to creep up on it, pop through its pickets, or simply grow in front. Nothing says rigid and new like a lonely fence standing sentry in the garden. The one exception to this is if you are defining a lawn at the street. It's okay to have the lawn sweep up to it, but at one end or the other, try to have a place to plant roses or another vine to creep up.

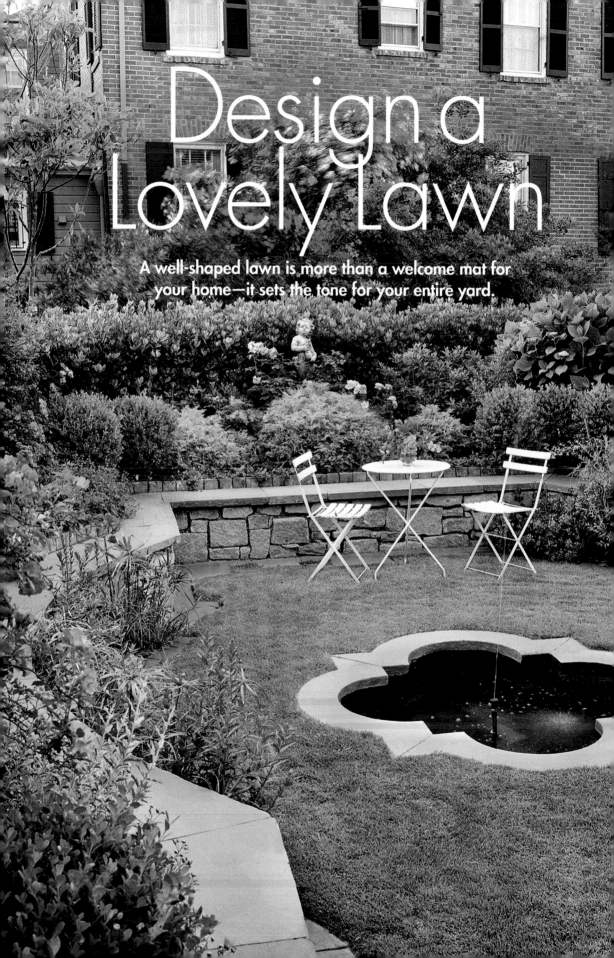

Design a Lovely Lawn

A well-shaped lawn is more than a welcome mat for your home—it sets the tone for your entire yard.

Shape Your Lawn

Most folks seem to have an endless carpet that runs from one lot line to the next. But a smartly shaped lawn can completely change the way your landscape looks—even before you plant the first shrub.

Fine-textured grass naturally gives the eye a place to rest. It also enhances what landscape there is and complements the bright colors of flowers. **Formal, straight lines** draw attention to every detail, especially architecture, and are well suited to flat areas. **Informal, fluid lines** move the eye around the garden and actually help camouflage imperfections. Start by assessing the architecture of your house. If the home's balance is symmetrical and your lot is flat, try formal, straight lines.

If your home has informal balance or a sloped lot, free-flowing curves are your best bet.

Whatever shape you choose, the line formed by the edge will have the greatest visual impact. It should be crisp and smooth. Curves should be broadly sweeping. The best way to get straight lines is to pull a string between two stakes. Corners should be square. For curved lines, practice with a garden hose. Once you get the shape you like, spray marking paint (sold at hardware stores) next to your line. If it's not to your liking, you can always start over. If you already have grass, use a shovel or sod cutter to remove all sod outside your line. This will become a planting bed. If you have no existing grass, establish your new lawn by laying sod or seeding. Turn the page for great choices for the South.

get the look

Do you live in a straight-line or curved-line city? The shape of a lawn greatly depends on topography, the size of the lot, and the type of architecture close at hand.

Flat topography, small lots, formal architecture: Charleston, Savannah, New Orleans

Flat topography, large lots, both formal and informal architecture: Dallas, Houston, Oklahoma City

Sloping topography, large lots, informal architecture: Atlanta, Birmingham, Charlotte

'Palmetto' St. Augustine

'Palmetto' St. Augustine

An emerald green color, exceptional shade tolerance, and fine texture make this low-growing, less-mowing favorite popular from the Carolinas through the Gulf Coast region. It also resists frost, cold, heat, drought, and bugs. Other great salt-tolerant St. Augustines to try are 'Sapphire,' a South Florida staple that withstands heavy wear and tear, and 'Captiva,' which is chinch bug resistant and stays low, reducing the need for chemicals and frequent mowing. Available only as sod.

'Empire Turf' Zoysia

A type of zoysia, this truly is a green grass and will earn you sustainable-design points. Once it is established, its genetic makeup helps it survive drought conditions. Slow growth means you mow less; it's also naturally resistant to chinch bugs because they don't like the taste. It is the only proven zoysia for Florida, and this durable yet soft-textured grass handles cold, too, making it good for all areas of the South. Available only as sod. Another great zoysia option: 'Zeon.'

'Empire Turf' zoysia

Centipede

This grass thrives in nonfertile, acid soil. Popular in the Carolinas and South Georgia, centipede is dubbed the lazy man's lawn because it looks great with little care—even better, it's also easy on the purse. Yellow-green in color, it has few weeds once established and readily rebounds after brief droughts. Never fertilize this grass more than once a year or you'll kill it. Start from seed or sod.

'Bella' bluegrass

'Bella' Bluegrass

Thanks to minimal vertical growth, 'Bella' reduces mowing by 50 to 80 percent. It fills in quickly and offers excellent injury recovery. Tolerant of both drought and heat, this dark green grass will make you proud if you live in the Middle or Upper South. Unlike other cool-season grasses, 'Bella' must be started from sod.

'Tifway' (T-419) Hybrid Bermuda

The most common grass used for lawns in the South (and also athletic fields). This deep-rooted, drought-tolerant, sun-loving turf is tough enough to withstand all that the neighborhood kids can dole out, yet it has a fine texture. Easy on the eyes, this grass does take moderate maintenance. If you love the look but want thicker grass, more shade tolerance, and less work, try 'Celebration' Bermuda grass. Hardy to the Upper South, it will also win brownie points for good behavior. Available only as sod.

'Tifway' Hybird Bermuda

lawn care 101

Whether you do it yourself or hire the service out, it's a good idea to know the basics.

Mow regularly, never taking off more than one-third of the blade at a time. If you let your grass get too long, it will shade itself, opening up spots for weeds to grow. Mow too close and the grass becomes stressed, making it more susceptible to disease, insects, and weeds.

Water responsibly. Established lawns do not need daily water, even when it's hot. Forgo spring watering altogether, especially if you're getting rain. Grass will develop deep roots naturally when it has to look for water.

Don't overfertilize. Doing so promotes disease and insect problems. Plus, you'll have to mow more often. Feed cool-season grasses in fall and warm-season ones in spring and summer. One exception is centipede. Feed it only once in spring. Use a slow-release product that's labeled for your type of grass.

Aerate your lawn in early spring. Well-oxygenated soil encourages microorganisms to break down minerals and organic matter to provide food for the roots. Rent a core aerator from an equipment-rental company to extract small plugs of soil from the ground. Though it will look like you've been visited by Canada geese, the plugs will disintegrate in about two weeks, lightly filling in any empty holes.

Sharpen mower blades at least twice a year. Clean cuts equal healthier grass.

Iceland poppies

plants you gotta grow

Plants are the accessories of our outdoor rooms. They are what brings form, texture, and color to your garden. There are thousands of different plants to pick from, so to help you out, we've chosen these as some of our favorites.

Flowering
dogwood

Eastern
redbud

Trees of the South

As your garden's largest living element, trees
have an enormous impact on the design.

Chaste
tree

Japanese
maple

Live Oak

No tree evokes this region's timeless grace and beauty better than a massive live oak *(Quercus virginiana)* draped in Spanish moss. Prized for evergreen foliage and colossal, widespread limbs, it's the perfect shade tree for suburbs, city streets, and country lanes. A live oak often lives for centuries, thanks to its strong, durable wood. Though it adapts to different soils and climates, live oak excels in the low, humid, rainy realms of the Coastal South.

Know it, grow it

Light: full sun
Soil: Live oak is adaptable, but it prefers fertile, well-drained soil.
Size: 40 to 80 feet tall, twice as wide
Where to grow: best in the Lower, Coastal, and Tropical South
Good to know: It drops leaves briefly in early spring.

Eastern
redbud

Saucer Magnolia

Giant, goblet-shaped blooms up to 10 inches across stand atop the leafless branches of saucer magnolia (*Magnolia* x *soulangeana*). Flowers are usually white inside and pink to deep pink outside. It's so eager to bloom, you'll even see flowers when the tree is only 3 to 4 feet tall. Smooth gray bark and plump, fuzzy flowerbuds lend interest in winter.

know it, grow it

Light: full sun
Soil: moist, fertile, acid, well drained
Size: 20 to 30 feet tall and wide
Where to grow: everywhere but the Tropical South
Good to know: Late frosts can damage the blooms.

Eastern Redbud

Though experienced gardeners love Eastern redbud (*Cercis canadensis*), it's truly a tree for beginners. It tolerates heat, cold, and drought. In early spring, hundreds of flower-buds pop from the leafless branches and even from the trunk. Flowers range from lavender-pink to rose-purple to white. Heart-shaped leaves may turn yellow in the fall.

know it, grow it

Light: sun to light shade
Soil: almost any well drained
Size: 20 to 30 feet tall and wide
Where to grow: everywhere but Tropical South
Good to know: 'Forest Pansy,' one of our favorites, flaunts leaves that emerge reddish-purple in spring and change to bronze in summer.

Saucer
magnolia

Crabapple

Prized for its handsome springtime flowers, crabapple *(Malus sp.)* also has fruit that is edible, showy, or both. Masses of single, semidouble, or double flowers with a musky sweet scent appear in spring, usually before leaves unfurl. Leaves are deep green to purple but don't put on a significant fall show.

know it, grow it

Light: full sun

Soil: prefers rich, well-drained deep soil but will grow in rocky soils and conditions ranging from acid to slightly alkaline

Size: Ranging from 6 to 40 feet tall, most top out at 20 feet tall and wide.

Where to grow: Upper, Middle, and Lower South

Good to know: Colorful fruit is showy in winter and attracts birds.

Flowering Dogwood

Considered by many to be the finest all-around tree, flowering dogwood (*Cornus florida*) begins its show in spring when 1-inch-wide, petal-like bracts smother leafless branches. White is the usual color, but you also can buy pink or red dogwoods. In early fall, its leaves turn brilliant red and crimson. Clusters of small, scarlet fruit persist into winter, supplying food for birds. It grows 20 to 30 feet tall with distinctly layered branches. Moist, fertile, well-drained soil is a must, lest its shallow roots fall victim to drought. Shade-grown trees bloom sparsely. You'll get more flowers in sun.

know it, grow it

Light: full to partial sun or light shade
Soil: moist, fertile, acid, well drained
Size: 20 to 30 feet tall
Where to grow: best in the Upper, Middle, and Lower South
Good to know: Named selections such as 'Cloud Nine,' 'Barton,' and 'Cherokee Chief' bloom better than trees labeled just "white" or "pink."

Yoshino Flowering Cherry

Renowned for its annual spectacle around the Washington, D.C., Tidal Basin, Yoshino flowering cherry (*Prunus* x *yedoensis*) forms soft clouds of snow-white blossoms in the early spring. The first of these cherries arrived in the South in 1912 as gifts from Japan, the tree's native land, and quickly became widely planted around the region. One of the reasons for its popularity is its rapid growth. A young tree can easily add upwards of 3 feet a year. Its spreading branches are superb for forming canopies over suburban streets or shading a large patio.

know it, grow it

Light: full or partial sun
Soil: fertile, well drained
Size: 30 feet tall and wide
Where to grow: Upper, Middle, and Lower South
Good to know: You can prune blooming branches and use them in arrangements indoors.

Crepe Myrtle

Talk about a tree made for the South. Crepe myrtle *(Lagerstroemia indica)* loves summer heat, tolerates drought, and grows better here than anywhere else. Red, pink, white, lavender, or purple blooms appear for months in summer. In fall, leaves turn red, orange, and yellow. The tree's smooth, flaking bark glows in the winter sun. You'll find many

know it, grow it

Light: full sun
Soil: well drained
Size: 4 to 40 feet tall, depending on selection
Where to grow: best in the Middle, Lower, and Coastal South
Good to know: Don't cut it back to stubs.

pruning 101

For a beautiful tree you can admire in every season, follow these guidelines.

- Prune in late winter. February is ideal.
- Remove suckers at the base, crossing or rubbing branches, and branches growing inward toward the center of the plant.
- As the tree grows, gradually remove all side branches up to a height of 5 feet or so.
- Cut back to another branch, to just about an outward-facing bud on a branch, or to the branch collar (a swollen area where the branch joins the trunk). Never leave stubs.
- Try to remove unwanted branches before they get thicker than a pencil.
- It's okay but unnecessary to cut off old seed heads. Leaving them on won't affect blooming next year.
- Don't round off, or "hat-rack," your plant, cutting back all of its branches to the same height. This ruins the natural form.

our top picks

You'll find lots of crepe myrtles out there. These are some of our favorites.

'Catawba': Upright, small tree growing up to 15 feet tall and wide; deep purple blooms; orange-red fall foliage.

'Osage': Arching, open small tree growing up to 15 feet tall; light pink, long bloomer; beautiful chestnut brown bark; red fall color.

'Natchez': Vase-shaped tree growing up to 30 feet tall and wide; beautiful cinnamon brown bark; longest bloomer; orange-red fall color.

'Miami': Upright, small tree growing up to 25 feet tall; beautiful chestnut brown bark; orange-to-russet red fall foliage.

crepe murder

Don't do this! Cutting big crepe myrtles into "fenceposts" produces wild, weak growth and ruins their form. The only penance for this crime? Cut them back to the ground in winter, and start all over.

When its huge, white blossoms open in May and June, magnolia-lined streets fill the South with sweet perfume. During the holidays, the large, glossy evergreen leaves of magnolias are prime ingredients in wreaths and garlands. Best suited to those areas where temperatures don't drop below zero, Southern magnolia *(Magnolia grandiflora)* casts dense shade. Growing grass beneath it is difficult, so substitute mulch or a shade-tolerant ground cover. Our favorite selection is 'Bracken's Brown Beauty,' which is noted for its tight, pyramidal shape; cold hardiness; and lustrous green leaves with rusty brown undersides. It matures at 35 to 50 feet tall.

know it, grow it

Light: full to partial sun
Soil: fertile, well drained
Size: 30 to 70 feet tall, depending on selection
Where to grow: best in the Middle, Lower, and Coastal South
Good to know: It drops leaves throughout the year.

Goldenrain Tree

Here's a tree few people grow that's a gold-medal winner in our book. Goldenrain tree (Koelreuteria paniculata) becomes a handsome, rounded, medium-size tree that has few pests, tolerates drought, and takes both suburban and city conditions. It makes a fine lawn, patio, or street tree. Large, loose clusters of bright yellow flowers smother the branches in midsummer, followed by showy seedpods. Leaves may turn yellow to orange in fall. It seldom needs pruning, but when it does, do this in winter.

know it, grow it

Light: full sun
Soil: well drained
Size: 25 to 35 feet tall and wide
Where to grow: all Southern zones except the Tropical South
Good to know: It's easy to grow grass beneath it.

Chaste tree

Goldenrain tree

Chaste Tree

Name a small tree with blue flowers that isn't a lilac. Stumped? That's because such trees are rare, and it's why you should plant a chaste tree. The most common form, lilac chaste tree (Vitex agnus-castus), quickly forms a multitrunked tree. Large spikes of blue to purple flowers crown the branches in summer. Cut off the spent blooms before they set seed, and you'll get a second blooming. Unnamed seedlings vary in showiness, so we suggest one of the following selections: 'Abbeville Blue,' 'Montrose Purple,' or 'Shoal Creek.'

know it, grow it

Light: full sun
Soil: well drained
Size: 15 to 20 feet tall and wide
Where to grow: throughout the South
Good to know: Prune in winter to remove dead twigs and crowded branches.

Red Buckeye

Native to the Eastern United States, red buckeye *(Aesculus pavia)* shows off 10-inch narrow clusters of bright red or orange-red flowers in the spring. You'll find this native growing along riverbanks and streambeds, so it appreciates moist soil and blooms under the filtered shade of taller trees.

know it, grow it

Light: full sun or light shade
Soil: rich, moist
Size: 12 to 20 feet tall
Where to grow: Upper, Middle, Lower, and Coastal South
Good to know: Attractive to hummingbirds.

Tulip Poplar

A fast grower, tulip poplar (*Liriodendron tulipifera*) is a showy tree that is resistant to disease and insects. In late spring, tulip-shaped flowers high in the canopy attract birds with their sweet scent. Foliage, shaped like that of a tulip bloom, turns to bright yellow in fall and is a real showstopper. Garden centers may carry two slower-growing selections, 'Arnold' and 'Majestic Beauty.' The former has a rigidly columnar habit, useful for narrow planting areas. This selection blooms within two to three years of planting. 'Majestic Beauty' sports yellow-edged leaves.

know it, grow it

Light: full sun
Soil: deep, rich, well drained, acid to neutral
Size: 60 to 90 feet tall, 35 to 50 feet wide
Where to grow: Upper, Middle, Lower, and Coastal South
Good to know: Trees don't usually bloom until they are 10 to 12 years old.

made to give shade

These large trees are perfect for most home gardens.

- 'Allee' Chinese elm (*Ulmus parvifolia* 'Allee')
- Ginkgo (*Ginkgo biloba*)
- Sawleaf zelkova (*Zelkova serrata*)
- Willow oak (*Quercus phellos*)
- White ash (*Fraxinus americana*)

Tulip poplar

Red Maple

This shade tree takes its name from the early flowers it brings to the waning winter landscape. Red maple *(Acer rubrum)* is one of our most popular native shade trees. In fall, the leaves turn a brilliant red or yellow. Even in the Coastal South, where color change is minimal, red maple puts on a glorious show.

know it, grow it

Light: full sun
Soil: moist, well drained
Size: 60 feet tall, 40 feet wide
Where to grow: Upper, Middle, Lower, and Coastal South
Good to know: 'October Glory' and 'Red Sunset' are the best selections for red fall color.

Sugar Maple

For many folks, a sugar maple *(Acer saccharum)* in full fall regalia is the signature sight of autumn. Growing 60 feet or taller with a tidy oval or rounded shape, it first turns color at the top and then proceeds downward. Some trees turn a gorgeous liquid gold, but the most compelling specimens turn sunset orange suffused with peach. Use sugar maple to line streets, driveways, and country lanes or to decorate a large lawn. Keep in mind that it doesn't like poor soil, confined roots, road salt, or polluted air.

know it, grow it

Light: full sun
Soil: moist, fertile, well drained
Size: up to 60 tall, 40 feet wide
Where to grow: Upper, Middle, and Lower South
Good to know: Don't prune in winter or cuts will bleed sap.

Japanese Maple

There are about as many selections of Japanese maple (*Acer palmatum*) as there are Smiths in the phone book. Some grow tall and upright; others are short and cascading. One thing they all share, however, is blazing autumn foliage late in the season. Colors include scarlet, crimson, orange, and yellow.

know it, grow it

Light: partial sun or filtered shade
Soil: moist, fertile, well drained
Size: 6 to 25 feet high, depending on the selection
Where to grow: everywhere except Tropical South
Good to know: Leaves may scorch in hot, dry weather.

our top picks

Of the numerous selections available, here are some of the best-known Japanese maple trees.

'Bloodgood': Vigorous, upright growth to 15 feet. Deep red spring and summer foliage, scarlet in fall. Bark blackish red.

'Crimson Queen': Small, shrubby, with finely cut reddish leaves that hold color all summer, turn scarlet before dropping off in fall. Grows to 8 feet.

'Fireglow': Upright growth to 12 feet. Deep red to burgundy foliage that holds well even in the summer heat.

'Glowing Embers': Grows to 20 feet. Heat and drought tolerant with deep green leaves turning to shades of red and orange in the fall.

'Osakazuki': Leaves to 5 inches wide, turn from a rich green in summer to brilliant crimson red in fall. Grows upright, becomes wider with age; grows to 20- to 25-foot round-topped tree. Sun, heat, and drought tolerant.

'Sango Kaku': Known as coral bark maple. Young branches have red bark. Grows to 20 feet with yellow fall foliage.

Ginkgo

Among the oldest of all tree species, the ginkgo or maidenhair tree *(Ginkgo biloba)* saw the dinosaurs come and go. Today, it's a foolproof shade tree with outstanding fall color. The fan-shaped leaves simultaneously turn a shimmering golden-yellow. Then they drop in a single day. Ginkgo thrives in almost any well-drained soil and has no pests. It's an excellent lawn tree as well as a good street tree because it tolerates drought, road salt, and pollution. Plant only male trees, such as 'Autumn Gold,' 'Saratoga,' and 'Shangri-La,' because females produce malodorous fruit.

know it, grow it

Light: sun
Soil: well drained
Size: about 60 feet tall, 40 feet wide
Where to grow: everywhere except the Tropical South
Good to know: It grows slowly at first, then faster.

Bald Cypress

Native to Southern swamps, bald cypress *(Taxodium distichum)* may at first glance seem like an unlikely landscape tree. However, it is adaptable to wet or dry soil and is a good choice for street plantings where root space is often constricted. It has needles similar to those of conifers, but unlike most conifers, it is deciduous. A carpet of brown needles blankets the ground in fall. In winter, bare branches are decorated with tiny cones.

know it, grow it

Light: sun

Soil: acid soil, adaptable to wet or dry conditions

Size: 50 to 70 feet tall, 20 to 30 feet wide

Where to grow: everywhere except the Tropical South

Good to know: Develops knobby growths called knees, when growing in waterlogged soil.

American beech

'Winter King' Hawthorn

The hallmark of these deciduous hawthorns isn't their spring flowers, but their bright red berries, which appear in August. But it's not until the leaves drop in winter that they put on a show. 'Winter King' (*Crataegus viridis* 'Winter King') is among the most attractive and trouble-free hawthorns. Its silvery gray bark flakes off to reveal cinnamon color underneath, and its red berries last all winter.

know it, grow it

Light: full to partial shade
Soil: well drained
Size: 25 to 30 feet tall, 20 to 25 feet wide
Where to grow: Upper, Middle, and Lower South
Good to know: Branches are thorny; avoid planting in high-traffic areas, or prune off the low branches.

American Beech

Pretty in all seasons, American beech (*Fagus grandifolia*) boasts lime green foliage in spring that darkens to deep green. In fall, leaves turn an exquisite golden brown. Its smooth gray bark and sculptural form make a handsome focal point in the winter landscape.

know it, grow it

Light: full sun or light shade
Soil: slightly acid, moist, fertile, well drained
Size: 50 to 70 feet tall, 40 to 60 feet wide
Where to grow: everywhere except Tropical South
Good to know: Heavy shade and surface roots inhibit the growth of lawn or other plants underneath it.

'Winter King' hawthorn

'Coral Bells' azalea

Florida flame azalea

Shrubs of the South

Shrubs help keep the garden comfortable and livable. These Southern favorites help to define a garden's style.

Ben Moseley rhododendron

Flowering quince

Boxwood

A healthy, green boxwood *(Buxus)* looks about as dignified as a plant can be. It adds an air of formality and permanence to the landscape, taking center stage in winter when trees are leafless and then receding gracefully into the background in summer when flowers dominate. Its tidiness and ease of maintenance make it a favorite just about everywhere it grows.

know it, grow it

Light: sun or shade
Soil: fertile, moist soil, excellent drainage
Size: 2 feet to as large as 20 feet, depending on type
Where to grow: Upper, Middle, and Lower South
Good to know: Poor drainage leads to root rot, which causes part of the shrub to become light brown and die.

Winter Daphne

If any shrub can challenge gardenia for powerful fragrance, winter daphne (*Daphne odora*) is it. As its name implies, it blooms early, often in February, displaying clusters of waxy, sweet-spicy flowers atop a dense mound of handsome evergreen foliage. Excellent drainage is essential. Planting in clay is fatal. Our favorite selection is 'Aureomarginata.' It combines crimson buds that open to waxy, white flowers with deep green leaves edged in cream.

know it, grow it

Light: light shade
Soil: loose, fast draining, no clay
Size: 3 to 5 feet tall and wide
Where to grow: best in Middle and Lower South
Good to know: It works well in containers.

'Arnold Promise'
witch hazel

'Arnold Promise' Witch Hazel

Fragrant and colorful, 'Arnold Promise' witch hazel (*Hamamelis intermedia*) makes a great addition to the winter garden. Branches are blanketed with shaggy, golden yellow blooms that resemble eyelashes in spring. Its open vaselike form makes this a good shrub to plant ground covers underneath. Leaves turn orange and red in fall.

know it, grow it

Light: full sun or partial shade
Soil: fertile, moist, well drained, acid or alkaline
Size: 10 to 15 feet tall
Where to grow: everywhere but Tropical South
Good to know: Cut branches make pretty arrangements indoors.

Winter daphne

Chinese Fringe

This fast grower can fool you at the garden center. Chinese fringe (*Loropetalum chinese*) quickly grows from a one-gallon pot up to 15 feet tall and wide, and can hide your house. So choose one of these improved selections in the *Southern Living* Plant Collection: 'Emerald Snow' (3 to 4 feet tall and wide, green leaves, white flowers); 'Purple Diamond' (4 to 5 feet tall and wide, purple foliage, pink flowers); or 'Purple Pixie' (dwarf, weeping shrub, 1 to 2 feet tall, 4 to 5 feet wide, purple foliage, pink flowers).

know it, grow it

Light: full sun or partial shade
Soil: well drained, nonalkaline
Size: 10 to 15 feet tall, 6 to 8 feet wide
Where to grow: Middle, Lower, and Coastal South
Good to know: Prune lower limbs away for a nice small tree.

Bridal wreath

Flowering Quince

If you're looking for a foolproof shrub, this is it. Flowering quince *(Chaenomeles sp.)* is practically indestructible and offers many forms and colors. Some are low and spreading (3 feet tall and somewhat wider), while others grow tall and upright (6 feet or more). You can use flowering quince in much the same way as forsythia. Our top picks: 'Cameo' (low, salmon-pink), 'Hollandia' (tall, red), 'Jet Trail' (low, white), 'Texas Scarlet' (low, red), and 'Toyo Nishiki' (tall; pink, white, and red).

know it, grow it

Light: full sun
Soil: adaptable to most soils
Size: 2 to 10 feet tall, depending on selection
Where to grow: everywhere but Tropical South
Good to know: Plant in a mixed border, as shrubs are unremarkable when not in bloom.

Bridal Wreath

Bridal wreath *(Spiraea prunifolia)* in a Southern garden is a marriage made in heaven. Delicate white blossoms resembling miniature roses line its slender, upright branches in early spring. In fall, its diminutive leaves turn bright red, orange, and yellow. For extra impact, plant bridal wreath against a dark background, and also plant several together.

know it, grow it

Light: full sun
Soil: rich, well drained
Size: 6 to 8 feet tall, 6 to 10 feet wide
Where to grow: Upper, Middle, and Lower South
Good to know: Prune after flowering in spring.

'Cameo' flowering quince

Forsythia

No deciduous, spring-blooming shrub is more popular than forsythia (*Forsythia x intermedia*), also known as yellow bells. That's because it's inexpensive and easy to grow, and you can always depend on it to be colorful. Countless yellow blooms smother its arching branches in late winter and early spring. Forsythia makes a fine clipped hedge, informal screen, bank cover, or seasonal accent. Prune in spring after flowers fade.

know it, grow it

Light: full sun

Soil: adaptable to most soils

Size: 6 to 10 feet tall

Where to grow: Upper, Middle, and Lower South

Good to know: Branches can be forced indoors for winter bloom.

Sasanqua Camellia

When few other plants are in bloom, sasanqua camellias (*Camellia sasanqua*) are loaded with flowers. Though they have smaller and earlier flowers than their showier cousin common camellia (*C. japonica*), sasanquas tolerate more sun, heat, and a wider range of soils. Even when not in bloom, this handsome evergreen shrub forms a nice backdrop for other plants.

know it, grow it

Light: partial shade
Soil: moist, well drained, slightly acid
Size: 6 to 10 feet tall, 4 to 8 feet wide
Where to grow: Middle, Lower, and Coastal South. Upper South gardeners should look for newer cold-tolerant selections with the words "winter" and "snow" in their names.
Good to know: Though they respond well to frequent pruning, it is best to select a form that suits your needs.

'Dawn'

'Reine des Fleurs'

Common Camellia

This is the shrub most gardeners have in mind when they mention camellias. More than 3,000 named kinds of common camellia (*Camellia japonica*) exist in a remarkable range of colors, forms, and sizes. Plant in spring or fall. Mulch thoroughly to keep roots cool and soil moist. Established plants tolerate drought.

know it, grow it

Light: partial shade
Soil: rich, well drained
Size: 6 to 12 feet tall
Where to grow: Upper (milder parts, protected), Middle, Lower, and Coastal South
Good to know: Deer do not browse these shrubs.

'Red Ruffles'

White
'Gumpo'

'Formosa'

Evergreen Azalea

One of the most beloved shrubs in the South, evergreen azaleas set spring aglow with their showy flowers. Though the flowers last only a couple of weeks, these evergreens sport handsome foliage throughout the year and are popular along foundation plantings.

Southern Indicas are the azaleas of choice in the Lower and Coastal South. They can survive temperatures down to 10 to 20 degrees and grow tall and fast. Favorite selections include 'Brilliant' (red), 'Formosa' (purple), 'President Clay' (orange-red), 'Pride of Mobile' (rose-pink), 'Mrs. G.G. Gerbing' (white), and 'George Lindley Tabor' (pink). Some reach 4 to 6 feet tall, but others can keep going. Check the mature size before you plant, and if you are looking for a flowering, evergreen screen, this is a good bet.

Rutherford azaleas are bushy, compact shrubs that are hardy to 20 degrees. Favorites include 'Red Ruffles' and 'Pink Ruffles.'

Kurumes are some of the most common azaleas. Generally hardy from 5 to 10 degrees, they feature dense growth and small, glossy leaves and reach an average height of 3 to 4 feet. Most popular is 'Coral Bells' (pink), but other available ones include 'Hershey's Red,' 'Hinodegiri' (fuchsia-pink), and 'Sherwood Red' (orange-red).

Satsuki azaleas, hardy where temperatures don't drop below 5 degrees, include low-growing, late-blooming ground covers known as white 'Gumpo,' and 'Gumpo Pink.' Others in the group are 'Macrantha Pink,' 'Macrantha Red,' and 'Wakebisu' (salmon).

Glenn Dale azaleas can survive down to zero degrees. Heights and growth rates vary, so do your homework. Ones to try in this group include 'Aphrodite' (pale pink), 'Copperman' (orange-red), 'Everest' (white), 'Fashion' (salmon-pink), and 'Glacier' (white).

know it, grow it

Light: partial shade
Soil: rich, acid, moist, well drained
Size: 3 to 10 feet tall and wide
Where to grow: varies by type
Good to know: Plant early, mid, and late blooming selections for a succession of blooms.

'Piedmont'

Native Azalea

Unlike evergreen azaleas that come from Japan, these lovely, sweet-smelling shrubs are native to the South and deciduous. Native azaleas grow up to 10 feet tall with an open, airy form. Clouds of pink, white, yellow, red, or orange flowers with protruding stamens appear in spring or summer. Easy-to-grow kinds include Piedmont azalea (*Rhododendron canescens*), Florida flame azalea (*R. austrinum*), Alabama azalea (*R. alabamense*), and swamp azalea (*R. viscosum*).

know it, grow it

Light: sun to light shade
Soil: moist, acid, well drained with lots of organic matter
Size: 10 feet tall
Where to grow: everywhere except Tropical South
Good to know: They won't bloom in deep shade.

Rhododendron

Few plants pop in color like rhododendron. A single cluster of flowers forms an impressive bouquet including as many as two dozen individual blooms. At home in the mountains, rhododendrons have a reputation for being picky in our hot summers. "Ironclad" and "Southgate" rhododendrons are known for their tolerance of Southern growing conditions. Choose named types such as those listed below for great results.

'A. Bedford': lavender-blue with dark blotch
'Album Elegans': pale mauve fading to white
'Anah Kruschke': lavender-blue to reddish-purple
'Anna Rose Whitney': deep pink
'Caroline': light pink
'Cynthia': rosy crimson with blackish markings
'English Roseum': lavender-pink
'Janet Blair': pink, cream, and gold
'Nova Zembla': red
'Roseum Elegans': pinkish lilac flowers
'Scintillation': pink
From the *Southern Living* Plant Collection:
Southgate™ Brandi™: pink ruffle blooms
Southgate™ Breezy™: white with maroon blotches
Southgate™ Grace™: white

know it, grow it

Light: filtered shade
Soil: loose, acid (pH lower than 6.5), with lots of organic matter
Size: 3 to 12 feet tall and wide
Where to grow: Upper and Middle South
Good to know: Rhododendrons prefer growing on a slope, where water quickly drains away. If your yard is level, plant in a raised bed.

Blue ensign

Cynthia

Ben Moseley

Chinese Snowball

Laden with hydrangea-like blooms, a single specimen of Chinese snowball (*Viburnum macrocephalum* 'Sterile') can add oomph to the border or be trained into a small accent tree. From April into May (and even early June in cooler climates), you'll be rewarded with spectacular, softball-size blooms. These flowers start out lime green and then open to pristine white.

know it, grow it

Light: full sun to part shade
Soil: well drained, slightly acidic
Size: 12 to 20 feet tall and wide
Where to grow: everywhere except Tropical South
Good to know: Many viburnums are fragrant, but Chinese snowball isn't—a bonus for those with sensitive noses.

French Hydrangeas

Also known as bigleaf hydrangeas, French hydrangeas (*Hydrangea macrophylla*) are favorite plants that Southerners love to clip and share with friends and family. In the warm days of summer, big balloons of delicate blooms in blues, pinks, purples, and white seem to float up like magic from the lush green foliage of these shrubs. Mophead types look like big snowballs, and lace caps are more delicate. Choose mopheads for a bigger show, and lace caps for more subtle display. Dozens of selections are available.

our top picks

'All Summer Beauty': Repeat bloomer.
'Ami Pasquier': Pink and crimson blooms even in acid soil.
'Ayesha': Clusters of cupped flowers look like buttons.
'Blushing Bride': Rebloomer that opens white and deepens to pink.
'Endless Summer': Repeat bloomer.
'Nikko Blue': The standard blue.

Nikko Blue

budget solutions

French hydrangeas are easy to root from cuttings. First, take 6-inch tip cuttings in summer, and strip off the lowest pair of leaves on each.

Next, wet the cut ends, and dip them in rooting powder. Finally, stick the cuttings into pots filled with moist potting soil, and place them in the shade. They should root in 6 to 8 weeks.

'Kurohime'

'Fuji Waterfall': Lace cap with pendulous, double white blooms.

'Pia': Compact grower to 3 feet tall, deep pink blooms.

'Sister Theresa': Large, snow-white blooms, deep green foliage.

'Tokyo Delight': Blossoms feature tiny pink or blue flowers ringed by large white florets.

know it, grow it

Light: morning sun with light afternoon shade

Soil: rich, moist

Size: 4 to 8 feet tall

Where to grow: everywhere but Tropical South

Good to know: Blue flowers are produced in acid soil (pH 5.5 and lower), and pink flowers are produced in alkaline soil (pH 7 and higher).

Roses

The rose is undoubtedly the best-loved flower and most widely planted shrub in the South. Centuries of hybridizing have brought us a dazzling array of colors, forms, and sizes. You can choose from foot-high miniatures to arbor-smothering climbers. Flowers range in size from as tiny as a thumbnail to as big as a salad plate. Red, pink, and white are the most common colors, but you'll also find flowers in cream, yellow, orange, magenta, purple, lavender, peach, and bicolors.

Heirloom roses are time-tested, easy to grow, and usually quite fragrant. They can be used as hedges, specimens, masses, or climbers. Most old roses are shrubs ranging from 3 to 6 feet tall with similar spreads. Climbing, or "rambling," roses can cover 10 to 20 feet.

our top picks

'Marchesa Boccella': Almost always in bloom; pink; light, sweet fragrance.
'Old Blush': Common upright shrub with prolific pink flowers.
'Reine des Violettes': Fragrance alone is reason enough to grow this rose; violet.
'Souvenir de la Malmaison': A repeat bloomer that loves the hot, humid South; pink.

'Zephirine Drouhin': Thornless climber with repeat, magenta-red, fragrant blooms.

know it, grow it

Light: full sun
Soil: moist, fertile, well drained with lots of organic matter
Watering: regular watering is essential for good growth and flowering
Fertilizing: repeat-bloomers need repeated feeding; once-bloomers need less
Good to know: Roses that need little or no spraying include 'Knock Out,' 'Carefree Beauty,' 'Old Blush,' 'Souvenir del Malmaison,' and 'Zephirine Drouhin.'

rooting roses 101

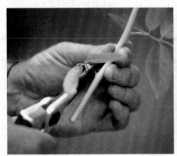  

Step 1 Take a cutting that is 6 to 8 inches long using sharp pruners. Cut at a 45-degree angle just below where leaves join the stem. Remove lower leaves from the cutting. Place stem in water to prevent it from drying out. (Fall is the ideal time to take cuttings.)

Step 2 Fill a small pot with moist potting soil. Pour a rooting powder in a small cup. Dip the cut end of each cutting in the powder. Tap the stem lightly to remove excess powder. Use a pencil to make a hole in the soil, stick cutting into hole, and then tamp soil at stem.

Step 3 Keep your cuttings moist but not soggy. Cover with a clear plastic bag for 2 to 3 weeks to retain humidity while they root. Most will root in 6 to 10 weeks. Leave in pots for several months. Transplant rooted plants into well-prepared beds in full or nearly full sun.

Gardenia

Few plants express the grace of the South as well as the gardenia (*Gardenia jasminoides*). Intensely fragrant, showy white blooms contrast beautifully with shiny evergreen leaves. Blooming begins in late spring and continues sporadically through summer. Our favorite selections include double-flowering 'Aimee' ('First Love'), 'Jubilation,' 'August Beauty,' and 'Miami Supreme.' Compact 'Kleim's Hardy' has starry, single blooms.

know it, grow it

Light: full to partial sun

Soil: moist, acid, well drained with lots of organic matter

Size: up to 6 feet tall and wide, depending on type

Where to grow: It does best in Lower, Coastal, or Tropical South. 'Kleim's Hardy' is okay in the Middle South.

Good to know: Whiteflies can be serious pests; treat with a systemic insecticide.

Lilac

herished for its flamboyant flowers, lilac *(Syringa vulgaris)* blooms in mid-spring, and its blooms are often fragrant. Long a favorite up North, it can be finicky in the prolonged heat of the South. Low-chill hybrids are a good choice for the South. Try 'Lavender Lady,' 'Blue Skies,' 'Old Glory,' and 'Angel White.' In the Lower South (Zone 8), you can also grow cutleaf lilac *(S. x laciniata),* littleleaf lilacs *(S. microphylla* 'Superba'), and 'Miss Kim' lilac *(S. patula* 'Miss Kim').

know it, grow it

Light: full sun

Soil: well drained, neutral to slightly alkaline

Size: 8 to 20 feet tall and wide

Where to grow: Upper and Middle South, some in Lower South

Good to know: Prune after flowers fade in spring.

Orange
sweet olive

Orange Sweet Olive

Sweet scented blooms and glossy green leaves make this versatile shrub a standout in the garden. Orange sweet olive *(Osmanthus fragrans aurantiacus)* can be trained as a small tree, hedge, screen, background, espalier, or grown as a container plant. Its fragrant orange flowers perfume the garden in fall. Give it morning sun and filtered afternoon shade to encourage blooms.

know it, grow it

Light: full sun or partial shade
Soil: adaptable
Size: 10 feet tall, 6 to 8 feet wide
Where to grow: Lower South, Coastal, and Tropical South
Good to know: Pinch out growing tips of young plants to induce bushiness.

Winged Euonymus

Also known as burning bush, winged euonymus *(Euonymus alatus)* is one of those plants that minds its manners most of the year but screams for attention come fall, when leaves turn a brilliant red. Plant in front of an evergreen backdrop for the most impact. It's a fairly large shrub, and there are several selections to choose from. Reaching 15 to 20 feet tall and wide, the species *E. alatus* can be limbed up and used as a small tree in the home landscape. 'Compactus,' the selection most often sold in nurseries, grows between 6 and 10 feet tall and wide. For something a little smaller, opt for 'Rudy Haag,' which maxes out at around 5 feet tall and wide.

know it, grow it

Light: full sun for best fall color
Soil: any well drained
Size: 15 to 20 feet tall and wide
Where to grow: Upper, Middle, and Lower South
Good to know: Winged euonymus reseeds readily in the Upper and Middle South and can be invasive in natural areas.

Winged euonymus

Pyracantha

A lazy gardener's dream, pyracantha *(Pyracantha sp.)* grows more vigorously if rarely watered and produces more berries if never pruned. In fact, because it bears its colorful fruit on last year's wood, any clipping done to keep it groomed as a hedge or espalier will reduce the number of berries produced. Selections offer red, orange, or yellow berries.

know it, grow it

Light: full sun
Soil: any well drained
Size: varies with species and selection
Where to grow: evergreen in Middle to Coastal South, hardy in Upper South depending on selection
Good to know: Plant only disease-resistant selections, such as 'Apache,' 'Mohave,' and 'Teton.'

Hollies

Hollies *(Ilex sp.)* are among the South's most useful plants for home gardens for many reasons. Many sport beautiful evergreen foliage. Most have beautiful berries. They offer a wide range of shapes and sizes from pyramidal trees to mounding shrubs. You can find them at almost every garden center.

These are tough, resilient, and generally pest-free plants. They adapt to many sites, soils, and lighting conditions. They also transplant well, and established plants tolerate drought. Some, such as winterberry, also grow in wet soil. Most evergreen species take well to pruning and shearing and make nice hedges and screens. They're also good in corner plantings by the house or planted out in the middle of a spacious lawn.

Foster holly

'Oakland' hybrid holly

With some exceptions, hollies prefer fertile, moist, well-drained, and slightly acid soil. Yaupon, possumhaw, and Chinese holly *(I. cornuta)* also grow in alkaline soil. Some hollies shown here lose their leaves in winter. They atone for this with magnificent displays of showy berries that ripen in fall and remain all winter—or, at least, until hungry birds finish them off.

know it, grow it

Light: full sun
Size: 3 to 50 feet, depending on species
Soil: Set in garden at the same depth it was growing in container. Prefers well-drained soil.
Where to grow: most places, but depends upon species
Good to know: Most types with showy berries need a male pollinator. 'Nellie R. Stevens' and 'Oakland' do not.

'Winter Red'
winterberry

'Afterglow'
winterberry

'Finch's Golden'
possumhaw

our top picks

American holly *(Ilex opaca)*: Makes a big tree up to 50 feet tall. Southeastern native. Takes pruning well. Red or yellow berries.

Yaupon *(I. vomitoria)*: Profusion of translucent berries. Southern native. Adapts to almost any soil. Grows 15 to 20 feet tall.

'Oakland' hybrid holly: Dense, pyramidal plant with oak-shaped leaves. Grows to 15 feet tall. Great for hedges and containers. Part of the *Southern Living* Plant Collection.

Longstalk holly *(I. pedunculosa)*: Berries form on long stems atop smooth leaves. Grows 15 feet tall.

Possumhaw *(I. decidua)*: Deciduous small tree to 20 feet. 'Warren's Red' has red berries. 'Finch's Golden' has yellow berries. Needs male pollinator, such as 'Red Escort.'

Winterberry *(I. verticillata)*: 'Winter Red' is best red selection. Pair with male 'Southern Gentleman' for berries. Deciduous. Grows 6 to 10 feet tall.

'Nellie R. Stevens' holly *(I. 'Nellie R. Stevens')*: Shiny leaves. Produces red berries without pollination. Grows 15 to 20 feet tall. Makes good hedge.

Foster holly *(I. x attenuata 'Foster #2')*: Conical plant often used for screening. Abundant red berries. Grows 20 to 30 feet tall.

Longstalk holly

'Yellow Berry'
American holly

American holly

Tulip   Bearded
iris

Bulbs and
Bulblike Plants

They may flower for only a few weeks each year,
but multiplied by scores of blossoms over a lifetime,
they make the garden rich with flowers.

Dahlia   Spring star flower

Summary Snowflake

Aclassic pass-along bulb in the South, summer snowflake *(Leucojum aestivum)* has been shared for centuries. Plants bloom November through winter in the Coastal South. Elsewhere they bloom with the early daffodils in late winter to early spring.

know it, grow it

Light: full sun or light shade
Size: 18 inches tall
Plant: 4 inches deep in fall
Where to grow: everywhere but Tropical South
Good to know: Plants need a little winter chill

Tulip

From barely blushing pinks and deep purples to every color in between, there's a tulip *(Tulipa sp.)* to please even the most discriminating gardener. Choose bulbs that are heavy and firm. Avoid any that are moldy or those that give to the touch. Plant en masse for the biggest show. In flowerpots, nestle them shoulder to shoulder for the most impact.

know it, grow it

Light: full sun

Size: 3 to 22 inches tall, depending on selection

Plant: 4 to 6 inches deep mid-October in the Upper South, December or January in the Coastal South

Where to grow: Treat the large-flowered hybrids as annuals. If you live in the Lower or Coastal South, buy your bulbs in the fall, and store them in the crisper drawer of your refrigerator, away from ripening fruit, for 8 to 10 weeks before planting.

Good to know: Can be planted in shade of deciduous trees, but good light should come from overhead; otherwise stems will lean toward the light source.

Spanish
bluebell

Hyacinth

Spikes of bell-shaped, fragrant flowers burst forth in spring and perfume the garden. There are two forms: Dutch and Roman. Dutch (*Hyacinthus orientalis*) is showier and fuller and comes in nearly every color. Roman (*H. o. albulus*) has more slender stems and delicate blooms. It is earlier to bloom than Dutch and is better adapted to the Lower South.

know it, grow it

Light: full sun or partial shade
Size: 12 inches tall
Plant: Set large bulbs 6 inches deep, 4 inches for small in October to December. Refrigerate for 10 to 12 weeks before planting in Lower and Coastal South.
Where to grow: everywhere but Tropical South
Good to know: The sweet fragrance of hyacinths is a treat outdoors but can be overpowering indoors.

Spanish Bluebell

The best spring bulb no one seems to know about, Spanish bluebell (*Hyacinthoides hispanica*) spreads steadily into glorious sweeps. It comes in white, pink, and blue. Blue 'Excelsior,' which dates back to 1906, is a standout.

know it, grow it

Light: full sun or light shade
Size: 15 to 20 inches tall
Plant: 3 inches deep in fall
Where to grow: everywhere but Tropical South
Good to know: The inch-wide, straplike leaves can look a little ratty before they die back, so plant in a mixed border to camouflage.

Hyacinth

Bearded Iris

These powerfully scented perennials make great cut flowers and come in every color of the rainbow. Enjoy their perfume and beauty both indoors and out in spring. Bearded irises grow from large, fleshy roots called rhizomes. Excellent drainage and full sun are musts.

know it, grow it

Light: full sun
Size: up to 4 feet tall
Plant: Space plants 1 to 2 feet apart in fall, and barely cover fleshy roots with soil.
Where to grow: everywhere but Tropical South
Good to know: In poorly drained soil, substitute Japanese or Louisiana irises.

Spider Lily

Easy to grow, spider lily *(Lycoris radiata)* spreads into drifts and lasts for generations. In August and September, tall spikes of flowers with long stamens that resemble spider legs appear seemingly overnight. Spider lilies send up foliage in the fall, which remains through spring, and then disappears.

know it, grow it

Light: full sun or light shade
Size: 18 inches tall
Plant: 3 to 4 inches deep in good soil
Where to grow: everywhere
Good to know: If planting in pots, set bulbs with tops exposed. Don't use pots that are too large; plants with crowded roots bloom best.

Lily-of-the-Nile

Spider lily

Lily-of-the-Nile

Lily-of-the-Nile *(Agapanthus africanus)* sports vibrant clusters of blue, purple, or white flowers atop deep green straplike foliage in summer. Each bloom cluster resembles a burst of fireworks. Massed plantings are spectacular.

know it, grow it

Light: full sun or light shade
Size: 18 inches tall
Plant: 2 inches deep, and 4 to 6 inches apart in well-drained soil
Where to grow: Lower, Coastal, and Tropical South. Elsewhere, grow in containers and bring inside for winter.
Good to know: Plants thrive with regular water, but once established can tolerate drought.

Oriental Hybrid Lilies

The most exotic of lilies, Oriental hybrids bloom from midsummer to fall with huge flowers of pink or white, often spotted with gold and shaded or banded with red. Pure white 'Casablanca,' rose-red 'Stargazer,' and white- and red-spotted 'Muscadet' top our list.

know it, grow it

Light: morning sun with afternoon shade
Size: 2 to 4½ feet tall
Plant: 8 inches deep and 4 to 6 inches apart in well-drained soil
Where to grow: all zones
Good to know: Plant bulbs as soon as possible after you get them; they do not store well. If you must delay, store them in a cool place.

Easter Lily

Often forced into early bloom in spring, Easter lily (*Lilium longiflorum*) naturally blooms in summer and flaunts large, trumpet-shaped white flowers.

know it, grow it

Light: morning sun with afternoon shade
Size: 1 to 1½ feet tall
Plant: twice as deep as the height of the bulb in loose, fast-draining soil
Where to grow: everywhere
Good to know: If you receive one at Easter, add it to your garden after you have enjoyed its display inside. Once the flowers fade, remove the plant from its pot, and place it in a sunny, well-drained location. Be sure to plant the bulb in the soil at the same depth it was planted in its pot. The bulb will then settle back into its normal bloom sequence.

'Muscadet' lily

Easter lily

Amaryllis

These bulbs are often seen at Christmas for forcing indoors. In the Lower, Coastal, and Tropical South, amaryllis (*Hippeastrum* hybrids) bloom in spring outdoors. Saint Joseph's lily (*H.* x *johnsonii*) is an early red-and-white hybrid that is popular in old gardens of the South. Tough and resilient, it blooms well in sun or light shade.

know it, grow it

Light: full sun or light shade
Size: 2 feet tall
Plant: In pots, set upper half of bulb above the soil; prefers rich, fast-draining soil.
Where to grow: Lower, Coastal, and Tropical South, or indoors
Good to know: Can be grown in pots. Water regularly during growth and bloom. When flowers fade, cut off stem and water as usual. When leaves start to yellow, let plants dry out, and repot in late fall or early winter.

Crinum lily

Amaryllis

Crinum Lily

Add this tough-as-nails bulb to your garden, and you'll be rewarded for years to come. A relative of the amaryllis, crinum (*Crinum sp.*) blooms from spring to fall usually after a rain. When a flower fades, you can just snap it off, and new buds will keep opening up. Flowers may be white, pink, or rose-red. Most hybrids do just fine from the Middle South on down. In the Upper South, stick with hardy crinum (*Crinum bulbispermum*), longneck crinum (*C. moorei*), and selections of *C.* x *powellii*. Mulching them in late fall provides extra insurance.

know it, grow it

Light: full sun or partial shade
Size: 2 to 6 feet tall, depending on selection
Plant: Set neck of bulb above soil, and space a foot apart.
Where to grow: Middle, Lower, Coastal, and Tropical South, or indoors
Good to know: Plant crinums where you won't have to move them. Once established, the bulbs can weigh 20 pounds or more.

Byzantine
gladiolus

Canna Lily

With leaves resembling those of bananas and spikes of showy flowers, canna lilies *(Canna sp.)* lend a tropical touch to the garden. Cut each flower stalk to the ground after it finishes blooming; new ones will appear and flower into early fall. In the Lower, Coastal, and Tropical South, plants will over-winter. Elsewhere, lift the rhizomes in fall, and store indoors until spring. Divide clumps every three or four years. Make sure each piece of rhizome has a bud or "eye," or it may not grow.

know it, grow it

Light: full sun

Size: 4 to 7 feet tall and 3 to 4 feet wide

Plant: 5 inches deep and 10 inches apart in rich soil, after danger of frost has passed

Where to grow: Lower, Coastal, and Tropical South. Dig and store rhizomes in Upper and Middle South.

Good to know: Ragged and dull foliage tells you that they're hungry, so feed plants weekly with a water-soluble 20-20-20 fertilizer. They will soon perk up.

Byzantine Gladiolus

An old Southern favorite, Byzantine Gladiolus *(Gladiolus communis byzantinus)* grows on 2- to 3- foot stems and make superb cut flowers. Left alone, they naturalize readily to form large sweeps of gaudy magenta blooms.

know it, grow it

Light: full sun

Size: 2 to 3 feet tall

Plant: Set corms four times deeper than their height and 4 to 6 inches apart in fertile well-drained soil.

Where to grow: everywhere but Upper South

Good to know: Plant behind mounding plants to cover leggy stems.

'Bengal Tiger' canna lily

Caladium

Native to tropical America, caladiums are prized, not for flowers, but for marvelous foliage—large, arrow-shaped leaves banded with red, pink, white, silver, and bronze. Grown from lumpy tubers, they make excellent bedding and container plants. Caladiums need rich soil, high humidity, and heat. Keep plants well watered throughout the summer. When leaves become ratty in late summer or fall, cut them back. The tubers won't take freezing weather and need to be stored inside during winter everywhere except the Tropical South.

know it, grow it

Light: shade to partial shade
Size: 2 feet tall
Plant: Place tubers knobby side up with tops level with soil surface, a foot apart in rich soil in spring when temperatures rise into the 70s.
Where to grow: everywhere
Good to know: Juices can cause swelling in mouth and throat. Wash hands thoroughly after clipping foliage.

our top picks

Most garden centers sell the big, fancy-leaved types. Our favorites include the following:

'Aaron': white with green edges
'Fanny Munson': pink with crimson veins
'Red Flash': red with green edges and white spots

'White Christmas': white with green veins
'White Queen': white with red veins
'Freida Hemple': red with green border

Pineapple lily

Spring Star Flower

Blue, star-shaped blooms, 1½ inches across, give spring star flower (*Ipheion uniflorum*) its name. Use it for edging, ground cover in semiwild areas, or under trees and large shrubs. 'Wisley Blue' is a favorite bright blue selection.

know it, grow it

Light: full sun or partial shade
Size: 6 to 8 inches tall
Plant: 2 inches deep in fertile, well-drained soil in fall
Where to grow: everywhere except Tropical South
Good to know: Prefers dry conditions during summer dormancy, but will accept water if drainage is good.

Pineapple Lily

A conversation piece in the garden, pineapple lily (*Eucomis sp.*) grows on thick 2- to 3-inch spikes closely set with half-inch-long flowers. It's topped with clusters of leaflike bracts that resemble a pineapple. When flowers fade after summer blooming, purplish seed capsules continue the show.

know it, grow it

Light: full sun or light shade
Size: 1 to 3 feet tall
Plant: 5 inches deep in fertile, well-drained soil
Where to grow: Hardy in Lower, Coastal, and Tropical South. Dig and store bulbs in Upper and Middle South.
Good to know: Good as a potted plant indoors or out

Spring star flower

Dahlia

Dressier than mums and bigger than marigolds, dahlias *(Dahlia sp.)* grace the garden with voluptuous blooms, just right for fall arrangements. Cut nearly mature flowers in early morning or evening. Immediately place in hot water; let stand several hours or overnight. Save tubers from year to year by digging them up in late fall after the first hard frost. Store in a cardboard box lined with newspaper and filled with moist potting medium. Place in a dry spot that will not freeze.

know it, grow it

Light: full sun (light afternoon shade in the Lower South)

Size: 1 to 6 feet tall

Plant: 4 to 6 inches deep in fertile, well-drained soil, after danger of frost has passed and soil is warm

Where to grow: Upper, Middle, and Lower South

Good to know: Don't water until tubers sprout. Once you see growth, use a soaker hose to provide a good dose of water without harming delicate sprouts.

Ginger lily

Dahlia

Ginger Lily

Handsome, sword-shaped foliage and honeysuckle-scented flowers on 4- to 8- foot stems make ginger lily *(Hedychium sp.)* a great addition to the back of the border. Common ginger lily *(H. coronarium)* sports pure white blossoms shaped like butterflies. Hybrids offer blooms of yellow, orange, and peach.

know it, grow it

Light: sun or light shade

Size: 4 to 8 feet tall

Plant: 6 inches deep in fertile, moist, well-drained soil in fall

Where to grow: hardy everywhere except Upper South

Good to know: Remove old stems at ground-level after flowers fade for new growth.

Alliums

Giant, lollipop blooms ranging in size from tennis balls to volleyballs on leafless stems shoot up in spring. Most alliums (*Allium sp.*) have pretty purple blooms. If you prefer white, try A. stipatatum 'White Giant.' This late spring bloomer stands 36 to 48 inches tall and produces blossoms 6 to 8 inches wide.

know it, grow it

Light: full sun or partial shade
Size: 6 inches to 5 feet tall or more
Plant: 6 to 8 inches deep and 8 to 10 inches apart in fertile, well-drained soil in fall
Where to grow: Middle, Lower, and Coastal South (Dig and store or grow in pots in Upper South.)
Good to know: Deer and voles won't bother them.

Hardy Cyclamen

You'll often see florists' cyclamen (*Cyclamen persicum*) grown as houseplants in garden centers. Hardy cyclamen (*C. sp.*) is a smaller-flowering cousin that is perfect for rock gardens, naturalizing under trees, or as carpets under camellias, rhododendrons, and large noninvasive ferns.

know it, grow it

Light: full sun or partial shade
Size: 1 to 3 feet tall
Plant: ½ inch deep and 6 to 10 inches apart in fertile, well-drained soil June through August
Where to grow: Upper and Middle South (Try *C. coum* for Lower South.)
Good to know: Top-dress annually with light application of potting soil with complete fertilizer added. Do not cultivate around roots.

Elephant's ear

Hardy cyclamen

Elephant's Ear

Fast-growing, with leaves up to 2 feet across, elephant's ear (*Colocasia esculenta*) lends tropical flair to the garden. It can be grown in beds or pots and make a quick but temporary screen. The purple-black leaves of 'Black Magic' are a stylish statement in the garden.

know it, grow it

Light: filtered shade
Size: up to 6 feet tall
Plant: 8 to 10 inches deep in fertile soil
Where to grow: Lower, Coastal, and Tropical South (Dig and store or grow in pots in Upper and Middle South.)
Good to know: The bigger the tuber, the bigger the plant you'll get.

Snapdragon

Viola

Annuals

These flowering plants provide quick, nonstop color and come in a nearly boundless variety of colors, shapes, and sizes.

Impatiens

Zinnia

Poppy

Delicate, paper-like petals give poppies *(Papaver sp.)* the appearance of being fragile, but they're tougher than they look. There are several species that share the same graceful appearance and will reseed year after year. Shirley poppy *(P. rhoeas)* blooms in bright colors on lanky stems and develops strong plants wherever their seeds fall. California poppies *(P. californica)* is native to the West, and grows well in Texas and other areas where soil pH is high. Opium poppy *(P. somniferum)* is one of the best ones for the South. It grows 4 feet tall with flowers that are 4 to 5 inches across.

know it, grow it

Light: full sun
Size: 12 to 42 inches tall
Plant: Set out transplants in the fall or spring or sow seeds in fall in well-drained soil.
Where to grow: everywhere as annuals
Good to know: When using as cut flowers, sear ends of stems with a flame before placing them in water.

Foxglove

Few plants rival the stately spires of foxglove (*Digitalis purpurea*). Blooms of white, purple, or pink add height and drama to borders. In the Upper and Middle South, foxgloves are short-lived perennials or biennials. In the Lower and Coastal South, treat them as annuals.

know it, grow it

Light: light shade
Size: 2 to 7 feet tall
Plant: In Upper and Middle South, set out transplants or sow seeds in spring. In Lower and Coastal South, set out transplants in summer or fall.
Where to grow: everywhere but Tropical South
Good to know: After first flowering, cut main spike; side shoots will develop and bloom late in the season.

Larkspur

Foxglove

Larkspur

An old-fashioned favorite for its airy foliage and tall spikes of flowers, larkspur (*Consolida sp.*) is often found in cottage gardens and will reseed year after year. It makes a great cut flower, and because larkspur retains its color after drying, it's popular for dried arrangements.

know it, grow it

Light: full sun
Size: 1 to 5 feet tall
Plant: Sow seeds in the fall after the soil has cooled. Plants will sprout in fall, wait through winter, and resume growth when spring approaches.
Where to grow: everywhere
Good to know: In the South, larkspur will begin to fade as the weather warms in June. Keep it well watered, and it may persist for a few more weeks.

Geranium

You'll see geraniums (*Pelargonium x domesticum*) in pots on porches all across the South, but they also will grow in the ground. No matter where you plant, geraniums appreciate a little afternoon shade. Never let the soil dry completely between waterings, or the leaves may turn yellow.

know it, grow it

Light: full sun with afternoon shade
Size: 12 to 25 inches tall
Plant: Set out transplants in summer.
Where to grow: Treat as an annual everywhere but Coastal and Tropical South, where it is a tender perennial.
Good to know: To encourage new blooms, remove old flowers as they fade.

Impatiens

Geranium

Impatiens

The top-selling annual flower in the South, impatiens (*Impatiens walleriana*) bloom continuously in shade from spring through fall in just about every color except blue and bright yellow. Double-flowered types look like little roses. Mass them in borders, or grow them in pots, window boxes, and hanging baskets.

know it, grow it

Light: shade to partial shade
Size: 6 to 24 inches tall
Plant: Set out transplants after the last spring frost in fertile, moist, well-drained soil.
Where to grow: everywhere
Good to know: If they grow tall and leggy by August, cut them back by half. They'll be bushy and flowering again in a few weeks.

Dragonwing
begonia

Angelonia

Perfect annuals for the neglectful gardener, angelonia tolerates drought and doesn't need cutting back or deadheading. Spikes of pink, white, or purplish-blue flowers, resembling orchids, appear continuously until a hard freeze in fall.

know it, grow it

Light: full sun
Size: 15 to 18 inches tall
Plant: Set out transplants in mid spring or later in moist, well-drained soil.
Where to grow: everywhere
Good to know: Angelonias are deer resistant.

Angelonia

Dragonwing Begonia

Easy color and easy care, Dragonwing begonias can't be beat. Just plant one and stand back. Four-inch pots will quickly grow into plants 12 to 15 inches high and up to 18 inches across. Pink or red blooms cover the plants until frost.

know it, grow it

Light: morning sun with light afternoon shade
Size: 14 to 16 inches tall, 15 to 18 inches wide
Plant: Set out transplants in fertile, well-drained soil.
Where to grow: everywhere
Good to know: Fertilize regularly to get more flowers.

You can't go wrong with common zinnias *(Zinnia elegans)*. These annuals love heat, tolerate drought, and bloom from spring to frost. Flowers come in about every color except blue and purple. No plants make better cut flowers.

know it, grow it

Light: full sun

Size: 1 to 4 feet tall

Plant: Scatter seeds over the ground in spring or set out transplants May to July in well-drained soil.

Where to grow: everywhere

Good to know: The more you cut zinnias, the more they bloom, so enjoy a bouquet indoors.

Coleus

There is hardly a leaf color, shape, size, or growth habit that coleus hasn't mastered. Red, orange, yellow, or pink leaves. Huge, scalloped, frilly, or tiny leaves. A plant that creeps, a plant that stands tall, coleus does it all. Large, shrubby selections (up to 36 inches tall), such as 'Aurora' and 'Alabama Sunset,' work well in the back of the border. Creepers and spreaders, such as the Ducksfoot Series and 'India Frills,' are great for edging, filling in spaces between other plants, or cascading from hanging baskets and window boxes. While older types prefer shade, new selections have been bred to take sun. Look for "sun coleus" on the plant tag at the nursery.

know it, grow it

Light: sun or shade

Size: 1 to 3 feet tall

Plant: Set out transplants in rich, loose, well-drained soil.

Where to grow: everywhere

Good to know: Pinch stems often to encourage branching, compact habit. Fertilize regularly with 20-20-20.

Pansy

Coleus

Pansies and Violas

You definitely get your money's worth from pansies and violas (Viola sp.). Set them out in fall and they will bloom in autumn and again in spring. Pansies (V. x Wittrockiana) are larger in flower than violas and come in a wide assortment of colors. Pinch off faded blooms to encourage flowering. Violas (V. cornuta) sport petite blooms that don't need pinching. They're more heat and weather tolerant than pansies.

know it, grow it

Light: full sun

Size: 4 to 8 inches tall

Plant: In fall, set out transplants 6 to 8 inches apart in rich, well-drained soil.

Where to grow: everywhere

Good to know: Plants will bloom better if the soil is kept moist.

Snapdragons

Plant snapdragons *(Antirrhinum majus)* with pansies and violas at the back of the bed. One of the best flowers for sunny beds, snapdragons reach their peak in spring and early summer.

know it, grow it

Light: full sun
Size: 6 to 36 inches tall
Plant: Set plants out in early fall in the Lower, Coastal, and Tropical South, spring in the Upper and Middle South, in fertile, well-drained soil.
Where to grow: everywhere
Good to know: Tall selections are prized for cut flowers but need to be staked.

Sweet William

Snapdragons

Sweet William

The flowers of sweet William *(Dianthus barbatus)* cluster into showy balls that brighten the spring border. Choose from white, pink, crimson, purple, and bicolored blooms. Dwarf strains such as Indian Carpet make good ground covers.

know it, grow it

Light: full morning sun
Size: 3 to 24 inches tall
Plant: Sow seeds in late spring to bloom the following year, or set out transplants in fall.
Where to grow: everywhere
Good to know: Cutting spent flowers before they produce seed will keep the plants blooming longer, but the flowers must remain on the plant if you want it to reseed.

Catmint

Pinks

Perennials

These plants range in size and shape from small mounds to giant towers, and there are choices for every imaginable garden spot.

Angel's trumpet

Hosta

Hollyhock

Place these old-fashioned favorites at the back of the border. Some single-type hollyhocks *(Alcea rosea)* can reach 9 feet tall. Newer selections and strains are bred to be shorter. Chater's Double reaches 6 feet, and Majorette tops out at 2½ feet.

know it, grow it

Light: full sun

Size: 2½ to 9 feet tall

Plant: Sow seeds in August and September for next season's bloom.

Where to grow: everywhere except Tropical South

Good to know: For a second set of blooms, after initial ones fade in July, cut off flower stems just above the ground. Continue to feed and water. Roots will push out another flush of growth that will bloom in September. These plants are short-lived and need replacing every 2 to 3 years.

Pinks

Two highly perfumed groups are available: cheddar pinks and cottage pinks.

Cheddar pinks *(Dianthus gratianopolitanus)* form neat, compact mounds of foliage with erect flower stalks up to 1 foot tall. Our favorites include 'Bath's Pink' (soft pink flowers, blue-green foliage), 'Firewitch' (magenta blooms, intense blue foliage), 'Greystone' (white flowers, gray-green leaves), and 'Tiny Rubies' (tiny, double, ruby-colored flowers atop a 3-inch-tall, gray-green mat).

Cottage pinks *(D. plumarius)* grow taller and looser with flowering stems up to 18 inches tall above gray-green leaves. Top picks: 'Essex Witch' (spicy, rose-pink flowers) and 'Itsaul White' (white flowers, vanilla scent).

know it, grow it

Light: full sun
Size: 12 to 18 inches tall
Plant: Sow seeds in fall or early spring in well-drained soil, or set out transplants.
Where to grow: Upper, Middle, and Lower South; treat as annuals in the Coastal and Tropical South.
Good to know: Fragrant flowers will attract butterflies but not deer.

Blue phlox

Blue Phlox

Native to eastern North America, blue phlox *(Phlox divaricata)* have slender stems clothed in oblong leaves. These spring bloomers produce fragrant blossoms with color varying from pale blue (sometimes with pinkish tones) to white.

know it, grow it

Light: light shade
Size: 1 foot tall
Soil: good, deep soil
Where to grow: everywhere except Tropical South
Good to know: Grow these plants in a rock garden or as bulb cover.

'Sarah Bernhardt'

Peony

A favorite for cutting, flowers of peonies (*Paeonia sp.*) can grow up to 10 inches across and are often fragrant. Choose from white and rose to red colors.

Peony flowers and foliage emerge from large buds or "eyes" on tuberous roots. In the Upper and Middle South, the eye should be covered by an inch of soil. But in the Lower South, place it barely beneath the surface. Mulch peonies in the spring to cool the roots and retain moisture.

Choose a sunny, well-drained spot free from competing roots of nearby trees and shrubs. Add copius amounts of organic matter to the soil before planting. Heat-tolerant selections for the South include 'Festiva Maxima,' 'Kansas,' and 'Sarah Bernhardt.'

know it, grow it

Light: afternoon shade

Size: 3 to 4 feet tall and wide

Plant: Plant rhizomes in spring no more than 1 inch deep in moist, fertile, well-drained soil that contains lots of organic matter. Pick a good spot because peonies don't like being moved.

Where to grow: Upper, Middle, and Lower South

Good to know: Cut flowers just as buds begin to open. Leave at least three leaves on every cut stem, and do not remove more than half the blooms from any clump. This preserves leaf growth that nourishes the plant for the next year.

Lenten Rose

Hellebores, or Lenten roses *(Helleborus orientalis)*, get their ecclesiastical nickname from their growing season. It begins in winter and extends into spring, surrounding the season of Lent. They make a hardy evergreen ground cover in shaded areas. Naturally drought tolerant, Lenten rose endures the summer, then puts on a flush of new growth in fall and again after flowers appear in late winter and early spring.

know it, grow it

Light: light shade
Size: 12 inches tall
Plant: Set out transplants in fertile, well-drained soil in fall. Space plants 30 to 36 inches apart. The crown of the plant should be sitting on the surface of the soil.

Where to grow: Upper, Middle, and Lower South
Good to know: After flowers fade, seedpods form. Let the pods turn brown and open before you remove them. They'll scatter seeds and give you free seedlings to transplant.

Hosta

Depending on the selection, hostas *(Hosta sp.)* form clumps from 4 inches to 5 feet wide. Leaves range in size from as small as the ear of a cat to as large as the ear of an elephant. They may be blue, green, yellow, variegated, smooth, puckered, quilted, rounded, heart-shaped, or sword-shaped.

know it, grow it

Light: light shade

Size: 4 inches to 5 feet wide

Plant: Plant rhizomes in rich, moist, well-drained soil that contains a lot of organic matter.

Where to grow: everywhere except Tropical South

Good to know: Our favorites for beginners include 'August Moon' (chartreuse leaves; white blooms; 20 inches tall and 30 inches wide); 'Golden Tiara' (small, heart-shaped leaves with gold edges; purple flowers; grows 12 inches tall and 15 inches wide); 'Halcyon' (heart-shaped, powder blue leaves; blue flowers; grows 18 inches tall and 3 feet wide); 'Royal Standard' (deeply veined, green leaves; fragrant, white blooms; grows 2 feet tall and 3 to 4 feet wide).

Solomon's seal

Solomon's Seal

Plant Solomon's seal *(Polygonatum odoratum)* for a pretty addition to a woodland garden. Small, bell-shaped blooms hang beneath stems on threadlike stalks in spring, followed by blue-black berries. Leaves and stems turn bright yellow in fall before the plant dies down for winter. 'Variegatum' has white-edged leaves.

know it, grow it

Light: shade

Size: 4 inches to 3½ feet tall

Plant: Set rhizomes 1 to 2 inches deep and 2 to 3 inches apart in fall. Prefers loose, rich soil that contains lots of organic matter.

Where to grow: everywhere except Tropical South

Good to know: To get more plants, divide rhizomes in early spring. Can also be grown in contaniers. Established plants tolerate drought.

'Antioch' hosta

Ferns

Grown for their interesting foliage, these perennial plants vary in height from a few inches to 50 feet or more. There are several groups of these plants. Most spectacular are tree ferns, which display their finely cut fronds atop a treelike stem. These need rich, well-drained soil, moisture, and shade. Native ferns do not grow as tall as tree ferns, but their fronds are handsome, and they can perform a number of landscape tasks. Naturalize them in woodland or wild gardens; or use them to fill shady beds, as ground cover, as interplantings between shrubs, or along a shady house wall.

Cinnamon fern

know it, grow it

Light: full to part shade
Soil: moist, fertile, lots of organic matter
Size: depends on type
Where to grow: hardiness depends on type
Good to know: All ferns look best when groomed. Cut off dead or injured fronds near ground or trunk—but don't cut back hardy outdoor ferns until new growth begins because old fronds protect growing tips.

nonhardy ferns for hanging

• Boston fern (*Nephrolepis exaltata* 'Bostoniensis') does best in indirect sunlight.
• 'Kimberley Queen' fern (*N. obliterata* 'Kimberley Queen') does well in sun if given enough water.
• 'Dallas' fern (*N. exaltata* 'Dallas') also does well if you decide to move it indoors.
• 'Tiger' fern (*N. exaltata* 'Tiger') is a fast grower that produces bright green leaflets striped with gold.

Southern maidenhair fern

Japanese painted fern

Catmint

Heuchera

Although they bear delicate flowers, many recent introductions of heuchera *(Heuchera americana)* are grown more for their brilliant leaf color. Try 'Garnet' for deep red winter foliage, 'Lace Ruffles' for ruffled leaves that are silvery white, 'Pewter Moon' for purple leaves with a silver center, 'Ring of Fire' for silvery purple-veined leaves with small purple flowers, and 'Velvet Night' for deep bluish-purple leaves.

know it, grow it

Light: partial sun to light shade
Size: 12 to 18 inches tall
Plant: Space 1½ feet apart in moist, well-drained soil.
Where to grow: Upper, Middle, and Lower South
Good to know: Divide clumps every three to four years in spring or fall.

Catmint

You don't have to be a cat lover to grow this fuss-free perennial. Catmint *(Nepeta x faassenii)* is not particular about soil, can tolerate drought, and doesn't like too much fertilizer. Besides its easy care, gardeners love catmint for its loose spikes of lavender flowers in early spring and summer. Cats like nibbling its foliage and rolling around in it.

know it, grow it

Light: sun (afternoon shade in Lower South)
Size: 18 inches tall
Plant: Space 1 to 1½ feet apart for ground cover.
Where to grow: Upper, Middle, and Lower South
Good to know: If you find the spikes of faded flowers unsightly, cut them back; this may bring on another flush of blooms.

Heuchera

Cape plumbago

Blanket flower

Cape Plumbago

Flowers that resemble phlox decorate Cape plumbago *(Plumbago auriculata)* from spring through fall. In frost-free areas it may flower throughout the year. Choose 'Alba' for white flowers and 'Royal Cape' for deep blue blooms. This plant also needs good drainage. Young growth blackens and leaves drop in heavy frost, but the recovery is good. Be sure to prune out the damaged growth after the danger of frost has passed.

know it, grow it

Light: full sun
Soil: fertile, well drained
Size: 6 to 12 feet tall and 8 to 10 feet wide
Where to grow: hardy in Coastal and Tropical South; grow in pots elsewhere
Good to know: Withstands light salt drift from ocean.

Blanket Flower

Native to the South and Midwest, these easy-going summer bloomers feature daisylike flowers in warm colors—yellow, orange, and red. They thrive on neglect so put away the watering can and fertilizer. These plants love heat, have no serious pests, and are not fussy about soil.

know it, grow it

Light: full sun
Size: 2 to 4 feet tall, depending on selection
Soil: good drainage
Where to grow: everywhere
Good to know: These plants are easy to grow from seeds and make excellent cut flowers.

'Ecuador Pink'

Angel's Trumpet

An old-fashioned pass-along plant, angel's trumpet *(Brugmansia sp.)* has long found favor in the South's coastal and frost-free climate. Pendulous floral bells sway gracefully from sturdy branches, perfuming the air with fabulous scent. Gardeners in cooler climates can have the same results by growing one in a container. Before the first frost, move the pot to a heated garage or basement to wait out cold winter months. It will drop leaves, so light is not a concern during this rest period.

know it, grow it

Light: sun or light shade
Size: up to 15 feet tall
Soil: moist, well drained or in pots
Where to grow: Lower (protected), Coastal, and Tropical South
Good to know: Angel's trumpets are heavy feeders. Using a liquid, blossom-boosting fertilizer such as 15-30-15 or 10-50-10 keeps them producing flowers. Water with plant food at least every other week, or more often if you'd like.

'Yellow'   'Charles Grimaldi'

Ornamental Grasses

Beautiful, affordable, and easy to grow, these gems are easy to incorporate into your garden. Ornamental grasses look great beside any body of water, be it a pool, marsh, stream, or ocean. They also work well mixed into herbaceous borders. Most grow quickly, tolerate heat and drought, and have no serious pests. To get more plants, dig and divide clumps in early spring prior to the emergence of new grasses; some, such as sea oats (*Chasmanthium latifolium*), seed themselves with abandon. So either remove the seedheads before they mature, or plant such grasses in naturalized areas where they can spread to their hearts' content. Other grasses, such as giant reed (*Arundo donax*), ribbon grass (*Phalaris arundinacea picta*), and blue lyme grass (*Leymus arenarius*) spread aggressivley by underground runners. To control them, dig and discard unwanted new shoots in the springtime.

Maiden Grass

The many forms of maiden grass (*Miscanthus sp.*) are clump-forming plants that need little care. 'Morning Light' boasts dark green leaves with silver midrib; 'Purpurascens' produces bright orange fall foliage.

know it, grow it

Light: full sun or partial shade
Size: 4 to 5 feet tall, 6 to 8 feet wide
Where to grow: everywhere except Tropical South
Good to know: Showy plumes appear in summer and fall. Deer don't like maiden grass.

Maiden grass

Chinese pennisetum

Gulf muhly grass

Chinese pennisetum

Also called fountain grass, Chinese pennisetum *(Pennisetum aloepecuroides)* is among the most foolproof grasses for the South. It has long, narrow leaves and arching stems that bear fuzzy flower plumes resembling foxtails. Bloom begins in summer and often extends into fall.

know it, grow it

Light: full sun or partial shade
Size: 2 to 5 feet tall
Soil: not fussy, well drained
Where to grow: varies by species
Good to know: Excellent in containers, in mixed borders, as dramatic sweeps, and for bank covers.

Gulf Muhly Grass

Native to the Southeast, Gulf muhly *(Muhlenbergia filipes)* lights up the fall, as rosy-purple wispy plumes rise 2 feet above the foliage. It's also called sweet grass because of its pleasant fragrance, which some liken to the scent of freshly mown hay.

know it, grow it

Light: full sun or light shade
Size: 2 to 3 feet tall without plumes
Soil: well drained
Where to grow: Middle, Lower, Coastal, and Tropical South
Good to know: Cut plants nearly to the ground in late winter to encourage fresh new growth.

Confederate Rose

You can't get more Southern than Confederate rose (*Hibiscus mutabilis* 'Plena'), a shrub with late-summer and autumn flowers that change from white to pink to deep rose as they age. You often get all three colors at once. Shrubby or treelike in the Coastal and Tropical South, it behaves more like a perennial in the Lower South.

know it, grow it

Light: full sun
Size: 6 to 20 feet tall
Soil: well drained, slightly acid
Where to grow: Lower, Coastal, and Tropical South
Good to know: Cuttings root easily in water.

Russian sage

Confederate rose

Russian Sage

Each stem of this shrubby perennial is topped with a widely branched spray of small lavender-blue flowers. When Russian sage (*Perovskia atriplicifolia*) blooms in late spring and summer, flowers form a blue haze above the foliage.

know it, grow it

Light: full sun
Size: 3 to 4 feet tall
Soil: not fussy; grows in both wet and well-drained soil; tolerates drought
Where to grow: everywhere except Tropical South
Good to know: To extend flowering period, trim off spent blossoms.

'Mystic Spires' salvia

Royal sage

Forsythia sage

Salvia

For a dazzling display in your garden, try salvias. Also called sages, these plants became horticultural stars in the 1980s and 1990s. Botanical gardens and collectors have introduced scores of new species and selections from Mexico, South America, Eurasia, and Africa, along with superior forms of our native species.

Flowers range from white and yellow through pink to scarlet, and from pale lavender to true blue and dark purple; all are arranged in whorls of two-lipped flowers whether distinctly spaced along the flower stalks or so tightly crowded they look like one dense spike.

Many gardeners enjoy summer-flowering salvias, but lesser-known kinds, such as Mexican bush sage (*Salvia leucantha*), royal sage (*Salvia regla*), pineapple sage (*S. elegans*), forsythia sage (*S. madrensis*), and 'Van Houttei' scarlet sage (*S. splendens* 'Van Houttei') start to bloom in late summer and thrive as the temperatures dip in September and October. Barring a hard frost, they can fill your garden with color until November or December.

know it, grow it

Light: full sun
Size: 1 to 6 feet tall
Soil: fertile, well drained
Where to grow: This large group of annuals and perennials will grow everywhere, but winter hardiness depends on species.
Good to know: These are among the favorite flowers of butterflies and hummingbirds.

A good companion for mums, asters (Aster sp.) bloom late summer to early fall and bring abundant color to a border. New England asters (A. novae-angliae) sound as if they would melt in our Southern summers. Not so. In fact, they're tough, dependable, and trouble free. Their blossoms resemble daisy mums in form, but asters usually grow loose and tall (good for the back of the border) and offer the blue and purple colors mums lack. Favorites include 'Harrington's Pink,' 'Hella Lacy' (purple), 'September Ruby' (red), 'Alma Potschke' (salmon-rose), and 'Purple Dome.' Frikart aster (A. x frikartii) is a favorite that requires excellent drainage.

Aromatic aster (A. oblongifolius) sports light blue-violet flowers that last through heavy frosts late into fall. Late purple aster (A. patens) tolerates drought and partial shade. Tatarian aster (A. tataricus) will grow in sun or shade.

know it, grow it

Light: full sun
Size: 3 to 5 feet tall
Plant: Space 3 to 4 feet apart in any well-drained soil.
Where to grow: Upper, Middle, and Lower South
Good to know: Divide vigorous clumps yearly in late fall or early spring.

'Hella Lacy'

'Cathy's Rust'

'Ryan's Pink'

Chrysanthemums

Some of the finest perennials for the garden, old-fashioned mums steal the show in fall borders. Excellent selections include 'Hillside Sheffield' (apricot pink), 'Cathy's Rust' (rusty peach), 'Clara Curtis' (clear pink), 'Country Girl' (rosy pink), 'Ryan's Pink' (soft pink), and 'Emperor of China' (silvery-rose pink). If you like mums that form tidy little spheres that are 18 inches across, don't plant these; they like to spread out.

know it, grow it

Light: full sun

Size: 12 to 30 inches tall

Plant: Space 15 to 18 inches apart in any well-drained soil.

Where to grow: everywhere except Tropical South

Good to know: Place taller-growing mums in the back of the border. Their flowers will fall toward the sun and hide any tired summer annuals that are planted in front. But if you prefer to have shorter plants, cut back tall growers by half in early July.

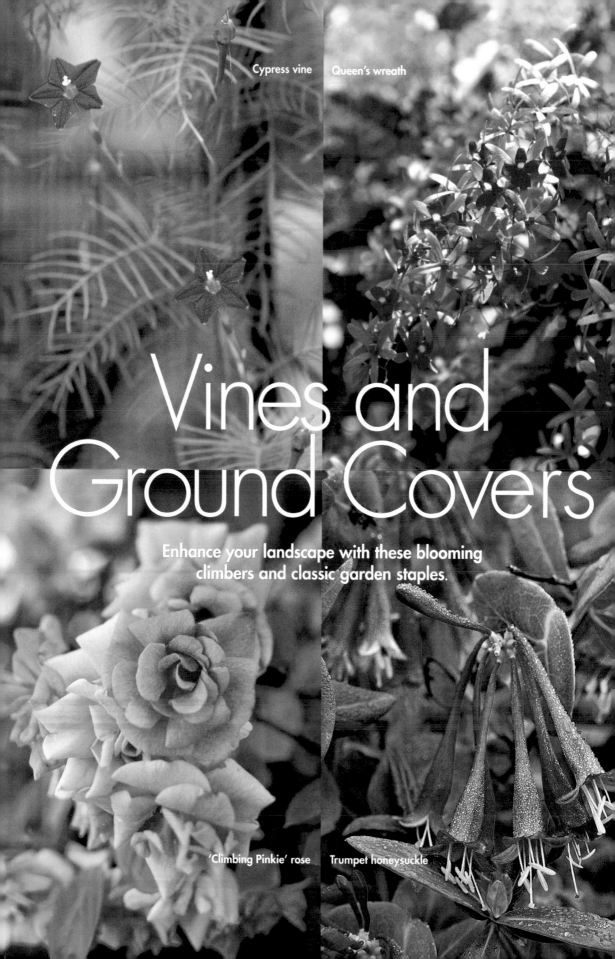

Cypress vine   Queen's wreath

Vines and Ground Covers

Enhance your landscape with these blooming
climbers and classic garden staples.

'Climbing Pinkie' rose   Trumpet honeysuckle

Carolina Jessamine

The state flower of South Carolina, this native vine appears everywhere across the South yet remains almost inconspicuous until early spring, when it bursts forth with bright yellow blooms. The funnel-shaped flowers of Carolina jessamine *(Gelsemium sempervirens)* produce a sweet perfume.

know it, grow it

Light: full sun; will tolerate light shade

Size: up to 20 feet

Plant: 6 to 8 inches deep in a sunny location; provide a trellis, mailbox, or fence for climbing, or let it ramble on the ground

Where to grow: Middle, Lower, and Coastal South

Good to know: This evergreen vine grows quickly but doesn't damage supports.

Clematis

If you've never grown clematis (say KLEM-uh-tis), you'll be surprised by the diversity of this plant. There are vigorous climbers and ground-hugging sprawlers. Some clematis have blooms as big as dinner plates, while others feature delicate bell-shaped flowers that look like fairy hats. Some are even evergreen, like Armand clematis *(Clematis armandii)* whose foliage is more significant than its flower. If grown correctly, clematis add romance and color to the garden, but in our climate, they can be tempermental. For success, follow these keys:

Keep in good soil. Dig a hole that's at least 18 inches deep and wide, working compost or manure into the soil. Add a handful or two of bonemeal.

Keep soil sweet. Once a clematis vine is established, sweeten soil annually by sprinkling it with a handful of bonemeal or adding a layer of wood ashes around the plant in late winter.

Keep it light. One of the best ways to lighten soil is to cultivate a healthy earthworm population. Using organic fertilizers is the equivalent to throwing out the welcome mat for earthworms.

Keep roots shaded. Maintain cool roots by adding a layer of mulch.

Keep it watered. Although you don't want to overwater clematis, the soil should be consistently moist throughout the growing season. This means giving roots a good soaking once a week. Clematis wilt, while caused by a fungus, is believed to be linked to water stress as well.

'Rooguchi'

'Madame Julia Correvon'

'Etoile Violette'

'Arabella'

pruning for perfect blooms

Clematis are divided into three groups that reflect bloom and pruning times.

Group I: Early (spring) bloomers. These are extremely vigorous and bloom on old wood (the prior year's shoots). Flowers are usually small and generally white. This group requires little pruning: Remove dead wood and then shape where necessary right after flowering.

Group II: Early and midseason bloomers that often repeat. These predominately flower on old wood, but some varieties will also flower on new wood (shoots that emerge that year). The group features larger flowers and requires more pruning than Group I. Once leaves begin to open, remove dead wood and shape.

Group III: Late (summer and fall) bloomers and the best for the South. Floriferous and showy, they take the heat of the day and tolerate warm nights. This group blooms only on new wood. They also require the most pruning, but it is the easiest: Cut back all of the previous year's stems to within 8 inches of the ground.

Note: If you are unsure which group you have, try this: Cut three to five stems back so that they are 2 feet long. Cut the rest back to 12 inches.

know it, grow it

Light: sun (Roots need cool, so mulch heavily.)
Size: up to 20 feet
Plant: The crown (where the roots join the stem) should be just aboveground. Make sure soil is well drained, and always amend with plenty of organic matter.
Where to grow: Lower and Coastal South for Armand clematis; everywhere but Tropical South for 'Yaichi' and sweet autumn clematis
Good to know: Begin fertilizing in spring when new growth emerges, and repeat once a month, stopping in fall. Anything labeled for roses or tomatoes will work. When planting clematis alone or in containers, stake them.

Confederate Jasmine

This evergreen vine is sometimes referred to as star jasmine because of the shape of its white blooms. In spring and early summer, the sweet-smelling flowers of Confederate jasmine (*Trachelospermum jasminoides*) can be seen encircling mailboxes, trellises, arbors, and fences. The versatile vine also works well as a ground cover.

know it, grow it

Light: sun or partial shade

Size: up to 20 feet

Plant: 6 to 8 inches deep in moist, well-drained soil

Where to grow: Lower, Coastal, and Tropical South

Good to know: 'Variegatum' has leaves bordered and blotched with white.

Creeping fig

Confederate jasmine

Creeping Fig

This enthusiastic grower will climb like crazy and cover a wall with tiny heart-shaped leaves in no time. Creeping fig (*Ficus pumila*) clings by aerial roots (sucker-like disks), so it doesn't have to be trained. However, it's not a low-maintenance choice as it has to be trimmed multiple times throughout the year to keep it in check.

know it, grow it

Light: sun or shade; not for walls with hot southern or western exposure

Size: capable of eventually covering a three- or four-story building

Plant: 6 to 8 inches deep in moist, well-drained soil

Where to grow: Lower, Coastal, and Tropical South

Good to know: Use only on brick or stone; it will ruin wood.

Climbing Roses

Let them sprawl on a fence, ascend a trellis, drape over an arbor, or scramble up a tree. Favorites such as 'Climbing Cécile Brunner,' 'Climbing Old Blush,' and 'New Dawn' not only bloom profusely in spring but also during summer and fall. Others, such as Lady Banks's, 'Albéric Barbier,' 'Russell's Cottage Rose,' and 'Veilchenblau,' provide one overwhelming display in spring.

know it, grow it

Light: full sun
Size: 10 to 20 feet
Plant: In moist, fertile, well-drained soil. Prune spring bloomers after flowers fade by shortening shoots that grow from main canes. Prune repeat bloomers anytime as needed.
Where to grow: everywhere
Good to know: Old canes eventually become brown, woody, and unproductive. Cut these off at ground level in spring to promote growth of new canes.

Crossvine

'Dortmund' climbing rose

Crossvine

A rapid climber, crossvine *(Bignonia capreolata)* is perfect for training on a fence or arbor when you need fast coverage. Hummingbirds love its showy spring flowers. You'll like its evergreen foliage.

know it, grow it

Light: full sun or light shade
Size: 30 feet or more
Plant: Dig hole as deep as plant is growing in container and twice as wide. Add organic matter to ensure soil is rich, moist, and well-drained.
Where to grow: Upper South (milder parts), Middle, Lower, Coastal, and Tropical South
Good to know: 'Tangerine Beauty' has exceptionally bright apricot-orange blooms.

Queen's wreath

Wisteria

One day, this plant just might gobble up the South. Wisteria *(Wisteria sp.)* is extremely vigorous and some types are invasive, but gardeners can't resist its lovely white, pink, or purple blooms. Each spring, long fragrant clusters of pea-shaped flowers hang from trees, arbors, or anything else the vine can reach. If you must plant wisteria, you may want to purchase American wisteria *(W. frutescens)*. This native is not as aggressive as Chinese wisteria *(W. sinensis)* or Japanese wisteria *(W. floribunda)*.

Chinese wisteria has escaped cultivation and consumed woodlands in the Lower South. If you plant Chinese wisteria, place it where you can confine it to a certain area. It works well in large containers and can be trained to grow in a tree form.

Japanese wisteria sports 18-inch-long flower clusters that open gradually, so it has a long bloom time. Like Chinese wisteria, it is aggressive, so be careful where you plant it. Do not allow Asian species to twine around railings, trellises, gutters, or small trees, as they will cause significant damage.

know it, grow it

Light: full sun
Size: 20 to 40 feet
Plant: Set in the garden at the same depth it was growing in container. Prefers well-drained soil.
Where to grow: everywhere except Tropical South
Good to know: Don't fertilize them too much, or you'll get all vines and foliage with no blooms.

Queen's Wreath

Clusters of purplish blue (sometimes white) flowers blanket queen's wreath *(Petrea volubilis)* several times a year in warm weather. It will take light shade, but the more sun it gets, the more blooms you'll see.

know it, grow it

Light: full sun or light shade
Size: 20 to 40 feet
Plant: Set a couple of inches deep and 3 to 4 feet apart. Not particular about soil.
Where to grow: Tropical South
Good to know: In colder areas of the South it can be grown in containers.

Wisteria

Morning Glory

Flowers that open in the morning and fade in the afternoon give morning glory (*Ipomoea tricolor*) its name. Showy single or double, funnel-shaped flowers come in blue, lavender, pink, red, or white with throats in contrasting colors.

know it, grow it

Light: full sun
Size: 15 feet
Plant: Nick seeds with a knife or file to speed sprouting. Plant ½ inch deep and 8 to 12 inches apart after frost has passed.
Where to grow: everywhere
Good to know: Perennial in the Tropical South; treat as an annual everywhere else.

Sky Flower

Use this fast grower to cover an arbor. Attractive heart-shaped leaves provide dense shade. Sky flower (*Thunbergia grandiflora*) sports blue blooms. For white flowers, try *T. laurifolia*.

know it, grow it

Light: full sun or partial shade
Size: 20 feet or more
Plant: Set in the garden at the same depth it was growing in container. Prefers rich, well-drained soil.
Where to grow: everywhere
Good to know: Perennial in the Tropical South; treat as an annual everywhere else.

Morning glory

Sky flower

Trumpet honeysuckle

Cypress vine

Trumpet Honeysuckle

Though it's not fragrant, trumpet honeysuckle (*Lonicera sempervirens*) bears showy flowers that are a favorite for hummingbirds in late spring and summer. Handsome foliage and scarlet fruit add to the appeal.

know it, grow it

Light: full sun or light shade
Size: 15 feet
Plant: Set in the garden at the same depth it was growing in container. Prefers moist, well-drained soil.
Where to grow: everywhere except Tropical South
Good to know: Will scramble if not given support.

Cypress Vine

This annual vine is a favorite of humming-birds and butterflies. Cypress vine (*Ipomoea quamoclit*) puts on hundreds of star-shaped, scarlet flowers in summer. Finely cut leaves resemble cypress foliage.

know it, grow it

Light: full sun
Size: up to 20 feet
Plant: Perform same procedure as for morning glory (see facing page).
Where to grow: everywhere

Bougainvillea

These tropical beauties are no longer restricted to the Coastal and Tropical South, thanks to low-growing shrubby types that can be purchased in full bloom in containers. Use potted bougainvillea *(Bougainvillea sp.)* on a patio as a summer annual and move to a protected area over winter.

know it, grow it

Light: full sun

Size: varies by selection

Plant: Roots are fragile, so it's important to keep the rootball intact while planting. Provide acid, well-drained soil. Heaviest blooming occurs in spring and fall (winter in Florida). To promote blooming, water and feed during active growth and let soil go dry in summer.

Where to grow: Coastal and Tropical South or in pots everywhere else

Good to know: Prune heavily after bloom.

Mandevilla

Bougainvillea

Mandevilla

This prolific vine twines around any structure, and its large blossoms are knockouts. Growing it in a container allows you to place it in the garden wherever it's needed. Plus, where it isn't winter hardy, you can take it indoors to save it for next year.

know it, grow it

Light: full sun

Size: 20 to 30 feet (less in containers)

Plant: Set in the garden at the same depth it was growing in container. Prefers moist, fertile, well-drained soil.

Where to grow: Coastal and Tropical South or in pots everywhere

Good to know: Feed every two to three weeks with water-soluble 20-20-20 plant food. Keep evenly moist.

Chinese Trumpet Creeper

If patience is not your virtue, plant Chinese trumpet creeper (Campsis grandiflora). It's guaranteed to provide shade in one season. Chinese trumpet creeper is not as vigorous as its native relative, common trumpet creeper (C. radicans). More reserved in nature, it actually makes the better garden guest, with big trumpet-shaped flowers in shades of orange, red, and peach from summer until fall.

know it, grow it

Light: full sun to partial shade

Size: up to 30 feet

Plant: Set in the garden at the same depth it was growing in container. Not picky about soil.

Where to grow: everywhere except Tropical South

Good to know: To control the size and stimulate flowers, which appear on new stems, cut back hard in early spring. Wear long sleeves and gloves because the flowers and leaves of this plant can irritate the skin.

Bleeding heart vine

Bleeding Heart Vine

Also known as glorybower, bleeding heart vine (Clerodendrum thomsoniae) boasts striking two-toned flowers. Large white calyxes surround scarlet corollas late summer to fall.

know it, grow it

Light: partial shade

Size: 10 to 15 feet

Plant: Set in the garden at the same depth it was growing in container. Prefers rich loose soil with plenty of water and good drainage.

Where to grow: Hardy in Coastal and Tropical South; take indoors for winter in pots everywhere else

Good to know: Plant is poisonous if ingested.

Chinese trumpet creeper

Ivy

Dependable, uniform, and neat, ivy (*Hedera sp.*) is a good solution for sloped sites that are dangerous to mow. Ivy will hold the soil and discourage slippage. Be aware, however, if given a place to climb, it will make its way up into trees and onto walls and fences. Algerian ivy (*H. canariensis*) is a good choice for the Coastal and Tropical South. Colchis or Persian ivy (*H. colchica*) grows everywhere and has the largest leaves. English ivy (*H. helix*) is not as vigorous as Algerian ivy but grows everywhere and is better for small spaces.

know it, grow it

Light: full sun to partial shade
Plant: Pinch off bottom 2 to 4 leaves, and set transplants deep to encourage more root growth. Space 6 to 12 inches apart.
Where to grow: everywhere
Good to know: When ground cover builds up higher than you want, mow it with a rugged power rotary mower, or cut it back with hedge shears. Do this in spring so ensuing growth will quickly fill in.

Mondo grass

Ivy

Mondo Grass

It's hard to imagine more serviceable ground cover for shade than mondo grass (*Optiopogon japonicus*). Plant it in large sweeps in areas where you don't want to mow or under large trees where grass won't grow. Use it to make a shady, low-maintenance lawn. Use it for its lush evergreen foliage; the summer flowers, borne on short spikes, are largely hidden by the leaves.

Monkey Grass

The South's favorite ground cover, monkey grass (*Liriope sp.*) is easy to find, simple to care for, usually evergreen, and tolerates heat. Throw in the fact that many types boast showy flowers, and you have a keeper. It's tough too. Tolerant of shallow soil, drought, dogs, and deer, these Asian natives can also survive the occasional crushing by car tires, bicycles, and a pickup baseball game. Little or no fertilizer is required. Select the right monkey grass, and your reward is even greater. 'Silvery Sunproof' takes full sun and combines green leaves with gold stripes and showy lilac flowers.

know it, grow it

Light: full sun to partial shade
Size: 2 to 12 inches depending on selection
Plant: Set finger-size sprigs about 8 inches apart; space larger clumps 1 foot apart in staggered rows so they will knit together.
Where to grow: everywhere
Good to know: Mow or cut back foliage to the ground before new shoots emerge (in March). If you do it after the shoots are up, the tips will be snipped blunt, and your liriope will be stuck with a ragged look for a year.

know it, grow it

Light: partial to full shade
Plant: Space plants 6 inches apart in well-drained soil.
Where to grow: everywhere except Upper South
Good to know: It's easy to obtain more plants by division. Use a sharp spade to divide clumps in early spring.

the edible garden

Kitchen gardens are popular again. For some, it's the romance of the harvest. For others, it's about being closer to the food they eat. Here we walk you through the steps for a successful garden brimming with vegetables, fruits, flowers, and herbs.

Backyard Bounty

Create your own kitchen garden. It's easy and economical.
Start small and expand your garden as your appetite increases.

There's no substitute for that just-picked taste of fresh vegetables.

Chefs know that the freshest produce makes the best meal. Anyone who loves to eat or even dabbles in the kitchen should take this to heart and plant an edible garden. If you're watching your pennies, start from seed. If you're the impatient type, go with transplants.

Start small. Even experienced gardeners Gene and Jan Harlow of Laurel, Mississippi, started with a manageable plot—the center rectangle (shown above). A few years later, the middle C-shaped bed was added, and it grew from there.

Grass paths between the vegetable beds give a tidy look and mud-free footing, even in damp weather.

tomato planting 101

Working from either side of the row, rake soil toward the middle, forming a mound. Use a rake to level the top. This will enable you to dig a deeper hole for your tomato plants.

Dig holes about 10 inches deep (about as wide as a small shovel) and 2 to 3 feet apart. Pour in enough compost to fill the holes, and lightly incorporate it into the soil.

Strip off all leaves halfway up the stems; plant the tomatoes so the soil reaches 2 inches below remaining leaves. You can also plant laterally with stems parallel to the ground.

Tomato supports keep the fruit off the ground. Here are our picks.

Tuteur

A pyramidal wooden trellis will add elegance to your garden. Use tuteurs in pairs for a more formal look.

Tomato Cages

Sturdy, galvanized cages fold flat for storage. Available in small, medium, and large sizes.

Simple Stakes

Economical choices for growing a lot of tomato plants. Choose from metal spirals or wooden or bamboo stakes.

From the Ground Up

Good soil is key to a great garden. If you are planting in raised beds, it's easy to tailor the soil to the plants you are growing. If planting directly into the ground, you'll need to add some soil amendments as well. Start with a soil test. The results will reveal your soil's pH (acidity or alkalinity) and also can reveal nutrient deficiencies. In some states, the Cooperative Extension Office can provide a soil test. If not, try a commercial laboratory. Soil test kits are available at many nurseries. Once you get your results, you can amend your soil accordingly. No matter the results, keep in mind that even good soil can be made better when you add organic matter. Make your own compost or purchase it by the bag. You'll find composted cow and chicken manure, humus (a mix of decomposed animal or vegetable matter), and even worm castings at your local nursery.

Recipe for Success

Add organic matter to the garden in spring and fall and whenever you put in transplants. Be generous with the amount. Add a volume equal to 25 to 50 percent of the total soil volume in the cultivated area. If you are gardening in a small space, you can work the compost in by hand. For larger areas, use a rototiller. (You can rent one by the day or hour.) Make sure you mix the organic matter in thoroughly. This will add air to the soil and amendments and help keep them in place. Repeat your soil test annually. Rotate your crops from bed to bed each season to reduce disease and soil depletion. Once your soil is right, it's time to get growing. Turn the page for some of our favorite vegetables, herbs, and fruits. For more in-depth information and plant profiles, consult *The Southern Living Garden Book*.

Nothing beats the taste of a homegrown tomato fresh from the garden. Here are a few tips to get you started. Choose a location that receives a minimum of 6 to 8 hours of direct sunlight. Support plants with stakes or wire cages. Be sure to anchor cages with small stakes to prevent them from turning over.

know it, grow it

Light: full sun

Soil: neutral to slightly acidic, well drained

Spacing: 1½ to 3 feet apart trained onto a stake or planted in a cage

Good to know: There are two kinds of tomato plants: determinate and indeterminate. Determinate types grow short and bushy and produce all their fruit at once. They grow well in cages and are ideal for canning. Indeterminate plants are tall and vinelike, needing strong stakes.

Our picks: 'Celebrity,' 'Floramerica,' 'Heatwave,' and 'Roma' (determinate). 'Early Girl,' 'Better Boy,' 'Big Beef,' and 'Lemon Boy' (indeterminate).

Cucumbers

Cucumbers

Vining types need 25 square feet to spread out on the ground, but you can grow them on a fence or trellis to conserve space. Bush cucumbers sport compact vines and are a good alternative if space is at a premium. Row covers will protect seedlings from various pests, including cucumber beetles and flea beetles. Remove the covers when plants start flowering so that pollination can occur.

know it, grow it

Light: full sun
Soil: loose, rich, well drained, evenly moist
Spacing: 1 to 3 feet apart along trellis
Good to know: Cucumbers taste bitter if the soil isn't kept constantly moist, so check the soil often. Seedy cucumbers have been left on the vine too long. Harvest every few days to keep the seeds in check.
Our picks: Slicers: 'Salad Bush' (hybrid), 'Straight 8,' 'Sweet Slice.' Picklers: 'Fancipak' (hybrid), 'County Fair.'

Eggplant

Few vegetable plants are handsomer than eggplant. Bushes resemble little trees, 2 to 3 feet high and equally wide. Plants are effective in large containers or raised beds; a well-spaced row makes a distinguished border between a vegetable and flower garden.

know it, grow it

Light: full sun
Soil: evenly moist
Spacing: 3 feet apart
Good to know: If you enjoy eating tiny whole eggplants, allow the plants to produce freely without pinching back growth or blossoms.
Our picks: There are many selections available from specialty retailers. 'Black Beauty,' 'Burpee Hybrid,' and 'Early Beauty' are good large choices. 'Rosa Bianca' is an heirloom selection with an attractive creamy white-and-lavender skin. 'Japanese' is a tender, more slender type that is popular with cooks.

'Rosa Bianca' eggplant

Okra

Okra

This heat-loving plant is ideally suited to the South. To speed germination, soak seeds in water overnight. Ants are attracted to okra but won't harm plants. Be careful when harvesting; the pod and leaves have prickly hairs.

know it, grow it

Light: full sun
Soil: well drained, high in organic matter
Spacing: Sow seeds ½ inch deep and 2 inches apart. Space rows 3 feet apart.
Good to know: Developing pods grow quickly. Harvest regularly, when pods are 2 to 4 inches long. Pods allowed to mature cause the plant to stop producing.
Our picks: For small gardens choose dwarf selections that top out at 3 feet tall, such as 'Annie Oakley' and 'Lee.' Good standards that grow to 6 feet include 'Burgundy' (its red pods reach 8 inches and are popular for eating as well as for drying and using in arrangements) and 'Clemson Spineless' (an old standby without ridges typical of most okra pods).

Garden Peas

Peas need coolness and humidity to thrive. In the Upper South, plant as soon as soil can be worked in spring. In the Middle and Lower South, plant in late summer for a fall crop. In the Coastal and Tropical South, plant around Christmastime. If you have room, grow tall (vining) peas on trellises. Bush types are more commonly grown in gardens and don't require support. Edible-pod snow peas and sugar snap peas grow in both spring and fall.

know it, grow it

Light: full sun
Soil: well drained, slightly acid to slightly alkaline
Spacing: Leave 2 feet between rows for bush types and 5 feet for tall vines. Thin seedlings to 2 to 4 inches apart.
Good to know: Peas have edible flowers, but if you pick them, you'll diminish your harvest.
Our picks: 'Alderman' and 'Multistar' (tall, vining). 'Blue Bantam,' 'Freezonian,' 'Green Arrow' (bush). 'Oregon Giant' (shown below), 'Norli' (snow peas). 'Sugar Daddy,' 'Sugar Pod II' (sugar snap).

Sugar snap peas

Peppers

Sweet peppers come in many colors—red, orange, yellow, green, and purple. You'll pay a fortune for all but the green ones in the store. Choose from bell peppers, banana peppers, pimiento peppers, and long Italian peppers. Hot peppers range in flavor from mild heat to scorching and in size from small, pea-size types to narrow, 6- to 7-inch long forms. Loosely tie young plants to bamboo stakes. Stakes will come in handy later as the peppers become top-heavy with fruit.

know it, grow it

Light: full sun

Soil: well drained

Spacing: 18 to 24 inches apart in rows 2 to 3 feet apart

Good to know: If plants stop bearing fruit in hot weather, don't pull them up. Keep them watered and tended, and they will produce again when the weather cools.

Our picks: 'California Wonder' and 'Yolo Wonder' (bells). 'Giant Marconi' (Italian). 'Habanero,' 'Jalapeño,' 'Anaheim,' 'Hungarian Yellow Wax' (hot).

Fresh Approach

Oklahoma City chef and organic gardener Kamala Gamble
shares her tips for tackling poor soil and for growing surefire
plants that even beginners can master.

Getting kids involved at an early age fosters good eating habits for life.

Kamala Gamble, the cofounder of Slow Food Oklahoma City, believes that meals made from naturally produced local vegetables, fruits, meats, and dairy are good for your health, the local economy, and your taste buds. So she decided to start her own organic garden. Here's what she learned along the way.

Start with the soil. Kamala enriched her black clay soil with copious amounts of composted cow and horse manure, green manure cover crops like alfalfa, and worm castings.

Mulching with hay also adds organic matter as it breaks down each year.

Edible Landscaping

207

easy starter plants

Kamala recommends the following plants for those embarking on their first vegetable and herb garden.

Basil: Plant in spring for summer harvest.

Why she loves it: "It's very productive, essential for pesto, and can be ridiculously pricey in the store."

Cucumber: Plant in spring for summer harvest. She grows hers on wire frames leaning against a fence for easy picking.

Why she loves it: She's crazy about the flavor of 'Lemon' and 'National Pickling' selections, and "they give you phenomenal production."

Leaf lettuce: Plant in early spring for spring harvest or late summer for fall harvest.

Why she loves it: "At the store, baby greens cost an arm and a leg, but you can sprinkle a packet of lettuce seed over the soil and have baby greens in two weeks. Plus you'll save $10 a pound."

Spinach: Plant in early spring for spring harvest or late summer for fall harvest.

Why she loves it: "It's nutritious and a quick grower that builds confidence."

Sweet pepper: Plant in spring for summer and fall harvest.

Why she loves it: "Let a green pepper turn red for sweeter flavor and more vitamins. 'Giant Marconi' produces like nobody's business."

Tomato: Plant in spring for summer harvest or midsummer for fall harvest.

Why she loves it: "There are a tremendous number of types, and they give you the most flavor 'pow' from your garden."

Cucumber

Eggplant and heirloom tomato

Heirloom Tomatoes

Varying in size, appearance, and plant habit, these represent old types that have been maintained by enthusiasts in different parts of the country. Tomato tasting is not unlike wine tasting. Different flavors appeal to different palates, and few crops offer a greater range of flavors than heirloom tomatoes.

To grow them, you'll probably be starting from seed. About 5 to 7 weeks before you plan to set out plants, sow seeds in flats or pots filled with light, seed-starting soil mix; cover seeds with ½ inch of mix. Place containers in a warm, sunny spot with a temperature of at least 65°F to 70°F; keep the soil moist. When seedlings are 2 inches tall, transplant them to individual 3- to 4-inch pots. If you opt to buy transplants, look for sturdy plants that haven't begun flowering or fruiting.

Squash

Squash

Squash

The most popular types of summer squash are yellow (both straightneck and crook-neck), pattypan (white), and zucchini (green). Plant squash seeds or transplants immediately after your last frost. Plant again several weeks later to extend the harvest.

know it, grow it

Light: full sun

Soil: well drained

Spacing: 3 feet apart on low mounds

Good to know: Blossoms and tiny delicate fruit of the female plant may be picked and eaten as a delicacy. Pick yellow squash when it's 4 to 6 inches long, zucchini when it's 6 to 8 inches, and pattypan at 3 to 5 inches in diameter.

Our picks: 'Early Prolific Straightneck' and 'Early Summer Crookneck' (yellow). 'Early White Bush' (white), 'Scallopini Hybrid' (green).

Grow Your Own Lettuce

Keep your salad bowl full with fresh, crisp greens from the garden. You'll be amazed by the selections available, and you'll save a bundle at the grocery store as well.

Lettuce

Most grocery stores stock gourmet lettuce, but you'll pay a small fortune for greens that aren't always the freshest. Save your money and grow your own. You can also add lettuce to a border mingled with flowers. Follow these 4 steps for success.

1. Choose the right spot. Plant lettuce in a location that receives direct sunlight for at least 4 to 6 hours. Plant in rich, well-drained soil. Amend clay soil with compost or finely ground bark.

2. Start with seeds. Lettuce grown from seed is economical and gives the greatest selection. Sow every 2 to 3 weeks to keep the harvest coming. Lettuce seeds germinate best in cool soil. Start 2 to 4 weeks before the last expected frost in your area. That's February in the Middle South and March in the Upper South. Lower and Coastal South gardeners can grow lettuce all winter, beginning with the first planting in October. (See page 262 for your climate zone.) Start with the more cold-tolerant lettuce selections in the cool months (see next page); then sow the heat-tolerant ones later to help carry you through the warming days of spring. Lettuce seeds require light to germinate. Sprinkle seeds on top of the soil, and lightly cover or scratch them into the bed just below the surface of the soil. Spray the seedbed lightly with water until seeds germinate. Lettuce must be kept moist throughout the

growing season. If the soil dries out, growth will stop, and leaves may become bitter.

3. Thin out plants. As seedlings mature, they need to be thinned. When they are 2 or 3 inches tall, gently pull out the largest plants. These will make your first salad; even though they are small, the leaves are still tasty. Leave about 6 to 8 inches between the remaining plants for sufficient room to mature. If pulling seedlings is difficult, pinch them off at their base instead.

4. Gather your greens. Expect to begin harvesting leaf lettuces 45 days after planting seeds and semi-heading selections in about 50 days. Pick outside leaves first; plants will continue to grow and produce. The new plants may not have the lovely form of the original ones, but don't worry—more leaves will appear. Or you can cut an entire plant 2 inches above its base. Lettuce is best eaten when it's freshly harvested; however, if you want to store it, soak it immediately in an ice water bath for 5 minutes. Then drain the lettuce and place in a zip-top plastic bag in the refrigerator.

keeping your cool

Most lettuce types will quickly 'bolt' (go to seed) and turn bitter in warm weather. Heat-tolerant lettuce last longer before bolting.

Cool-Weather Lettuce

- 'Buttercrunch' (green, semi-heading)
- 'Four Seasons' (red and green, semi-heading)
- 'Lollo Rosso' (red, leaf lettuce)
- 'Royal Oak Leaf' (green, leaf lettuce)
- 'Tom Thumb' (green, semi-heading)

'Black-seeded Simpson'

A heat-tolerant leaf lettuce, 'Black-seeded Simpson' is apple green with large leaves.

know it, grow it

Light: full sun
Soil: loose, rich, well drained, evenly moist
Spacing: Thin seedlings to 6 inches apart.
Days to Maturity: 40
Why we like it: Grows fast; mild, sweet taste.

'Black-seeded Simpson'

Heat-Tolerant Lettuce

- 'Black-seeded Simpson' (green, leaf lettuce)
- 'Craquerelle du Midi' (green, romaine type)
- 'Red Riding Hood' (red, semi-heading)
- 'Red Sails' (red, leaf lettuce)

'Red Sails' lettuce

'Red Sails' Lettuce

An All-America Selections Winner, 'Red Sails' has handsome, reddish foliage.

know it, grow it

Light: full sun
Soil: loose, rich, well drained, evenly moist
Spacing: 4 to 6 inches apart
Days to Maturity: 40
Why we like it: Slow to bolt; packed with vitamins A and C.

'Buttercrunch' Lettuce

A semi-heading type, 'Buttercrunch' likes cool weather but will tolerate some heat.

know it, grow it

Light: full sun
Soil: evenly moist
Days to Maturity: 55 to 60
Why we like it: Crisp texture; tasty leaves.

lettuce 101

The great thing about growing your own lettuce is the sheer variety available.

Leaf lettuce is the easiest type for home gardeners to grow. Instead of forming heads, it grows in loose rosettes. Good selections for the South include: 'Black-seeded Simpson,' 'Oak Leaf,' 'Slobolt,' 'Red Sails,' and 'Ruby.'

Butterhead or Boston types have loose heads with smooth green outer leaves and yellow inner ones. Try 'Bibb,' 'Buttercrunch,' and 'Mignonette.'

Crisphead is the most widely sold type in the supermarket but can be exasperating for home gardeners. Heads form best when temperatures average around 55°F to 60°F. Best types are strains of 'Great Lakes.'

Romaine sports erect cylindrical heads of smooth leaves. It tolerates heat moderately well. Try "Dark Green Cos,' 'Parris Island,' Valmaine,' or 'White Paris.'

'Buttercrunch' lettuce

Raised Right

Formal brick beds punctuated with urns and large-scale
planters dress up a kitchen garden chock-full of ornamentals,

Raised beds filled with a fertile mix of soil and compost help plants thrive.

Today's kitchen garden is a far cry from the rows of beans and corn your grandparents knew so well. Designed as a part of the landscape, these attainable luxuries are sophisticated and space savvy. Raised beds and containers make the process easier, ensuring a higher rate of success for the beginner. Jill and Todd Utz wanted their garden to be pretty and productive and brimming with ornamentals as well as edibles.

Raised brick beds add formality to the space and allowed garden designer Bryan Ramsey to add the right mix of soil for plants to thrive.

Paths within the beds are made of crushed oyster shells—a product often fed to chickens to aid digestion. Lower paths are mulched with bark.

Having It All

Kitchen gardens don't have to be a shaggy mess that must be hidden from view. They can be pretty and productive all in one spot. The Utz family's garden definitely raises the bar. We hope you will borrow a few of the great ideas and grow some goodness for yourself.

Wish list. Inspired by friends who frequently cooked with produce from their own garden, Todd and Jill decided to plant one for themselves and their girls. Before putting the first plant in the ground, the couple thought through everything they wanted in the garden. It had to be pretty, friendly for their kids, and they wanted it to be organic—a tall order for a not-so-large space. They asked John Fluitt, co-owner of Garden Design Associates in Oklahoma City for help. He plotted out a sunny spot behind the garage and started checking through the wish list. First the space was anchored with a pair of outbuildings—one for storage and the other a playhouse for the girls. Clay soil necessitated raised beds. Brick was a natural choice because it blends with surrounding architecture. A drip irrigation system provides water only where it's needed.

Plants aplenty. Flowers, herbs, fruits, and vegetables all live happily in the space. Parsley and bronze fennel are enjoyed by the family as well as several caterpillars that will soon turn into swallowtail butterflies. Strawberries, 'Celeste' figs, and dwarf 'Golden Sentinel' apples are picked and eaten right on the spot because they have been grown without harmful chemicals. Lettuce stars in salads spring through fall. Flowers pop up along the paths and soften the brick. Now the family can't even imagine life without their patch of paradise.

get the look

Materials matter. Raised beds can be made from a host of different materials including brick, pressure-treated lumber, stone, concrete, and even galvanized tubs. The key is to match the material to its surroundings. Here brick works to set a formal tone. Bricks turned on edge hold soil and gravel in place along paths.

Add ornaments. Bell jars, or cloches, set atop sunken pots become ornamental during warmer weather, but are used for protecting young starts when the air is chilly. Urns planted with ornamentals underscore the formal feel of the garden. Large pots used solely for texture and scale are left unplanted for a sculptural look. Finials add another decorative touch.

Think small. Dwarf selections of fruit trees grow well in pots and are the perfect alternative to large trees when space is limited. In this garden, dwarf 'Golden Sentinel' apples yield enough for the family and elegantly anchor the bed in symmetrically placed pots.

Make it pretty. Jill and Todd wanted their garden to be more than just a vegetable patch. Flowers such as purple asters and lacy yellow yarrows add color and charm. When planting flowers with edibles, choose plants that have the same sun and water requirements. Plant a few edible flowers, and toss them in with your salad for a pretty presentation.

design secret: Boxwoods, rosemary, and thyme keep the kitchen garden from looking bare when the harvest is over.

Easy-to-Grow Herbs

Growing these tasty plants is as much fun as cooking with them.

Chives

With clumps of grasslike leaves, chives (*Allium schoenoprasum*) are valued for their mild flavor and rosy-purple flowers in spring. They're especially easy to grow because they spread from both seeds and tuberous rootstocks. Scatter seeds in a well-drained garden bed that gets at least 6 hours of sunlight daily.

know it, grow it

Light: full sun
Soil: moist, well drained
Type: perennial
When to plant: cool weather
Good to know: Closely related garlic chives (*A. tuberosum*) have white blooms and a mild garlic flavor. However, they self-seed so profusely that they require cutting back to make sure they don't spread to every part of your garden. Grow them in containers to keep them at bay.

Basil

Basil

Just about anyone can grow basil (*Ocimum basilicum*), but deciding which one to try can be difficult because there are so many choices. 'Genovese' sweet basil is the best selection for making pesto or flavoring spaghetti sauce. Licorice-flavored 'Siam Queen' is perfect for Thai and Vietnamese dishes. Purple-leaved selections such as 'Red Rubin' and 'Purple Ruffles' look great in the garden and on the plate. Lemon basil ('Citriodorum') will surprise you with its citrus scent.

know it, grow it

Light: full sun
Soil: moist, well drained
Type: annual
When to grow: warm weather
Good to know: Several small-leaved dwarf types, such as 'Dwarf Bush Fineleaf,' 'Minette,' and 'Spicy Bush,' thrive in containers and can also be used for edging beds.

Chives

This musky-flavored herb resembles parsley. If you get them confused, plant cilantro *(Coriandrum sativum)* in a separate container. Use it copiously during spring; it doesn't dry or freeze well for later use.

know it, grow it

Light: full sun
Soil: moist, well drained
Type: annual
When to plant: cool weather
Good to know: Once evenings warm and days become hot, cilantro will succumb. Plant in early spring and again in fall.

Bringing as much to the landscape as it does to the palate, dill's *(Anethum graveolens)* finely textured blue-green foliage grows on upright, fountainous stems. In late spring, cut the chartreuse flowers and use them in arrangements.

know it, grow it

Light: full sun
Soil: moist, fertile, well drained
Type: annual
When to plant: cool weather
Good to know: Dill also produces pungent seeds that you can easily dry and store for culinary use, particularly for dill pickles.

Parsley

Flat-leaf parsley *(Petroselinum crispum)* produces the best flavor for cooking. The curly selection's slightly bitter taste makes it an excellent garnish or a decorative addition to the garden. (It's perfect with pansies.)

know it, grow it

Light: full sun
Soil: moist, fertile, well drained
Type: biennial grown as annual
When to plant: cool weather
Good to know: Once hot weather hits, move the herb from its pot to a spot in the garden with similar light conditions and well-drained soil.

happy herbs

Sun: Most herbs like a minimum of 5 hours of direct sunlight every day. Filtered light in the afternoon prolongs their life and flavor.

Planting in containers: Always use a good-quality potting soil. There are numerous types available, so keep the following considerations in mind when making your selection. First, cheap is not always the best choice. Also, choose soil that's light in the bag; heavy sacks can indicate soil that may not drain well. If your containers are small, consider a potting mix with moisture-retaining polymers already included. Place the soil in a clean bucket, and add water to thoroughly moisten. Loosely fill your container with the damp soil.

Fertilizer: Plant with a timed-release, granular fertilizer such as 14-14-14. In midsummer, use a water-soluble liquid such as 20-20-20. Do not apply blossom-boosting plant food.

Water: Keep soil moist and well drained. Herbs don't like wet feet. Remember, herbs planted in small pots dry out quickly, so consider using containers at least 12 inches in diameter.

Maintenance: Trim herbs frequently to prevent them from flowering. When they bloom, their flavor diminishes and growth of tasty new foliage slows.

Drying: Cut herbs and bundle stems with garden twine. Hang them upside down in a warm, dry place such as a garage. Once the herbs are completely dried, crumble and store in an airtight container.

Mint

Tough and unfussy, mint *(Mentha sp.)* can grow almost anywhere. Plants spread rapidly by underground stems and can be quite invasive. To keep them inbounds, grow them in pots on the patio or sink pots in the ground. Replant about every three years.

know it, grow it

Light: full sun
Soil: light, medium-rich, moist
Type: perennial
When to plant: warm weather
Good to know: Mint comes in a variety of flavors, from peppermint and spearmint to apple, orange, and chocolate. Try a few of each for an aromatic treat.

Thyme

Rosemary

One of the easiest and most fragrant herbs to grow, rosemary *(Rosmarinus officinalis)* is great for beginners. Give it full sun and well-drained soil, and this bushy perennial shrub will thrive. Selections vary in height from 1 to 6 feet. In the Upper and Middle South, choose cold-hardy selections such as 'Arp,' 'Hill's Hardy,' and 'Irene.' For superior flavor, try 'Blue Boy' and 'Blue Spires.' Unlike most herbs, rosemary has a stronger flavor when it's dried, so you'll need to use less when substituting for fresh.

know it, grow it

Light: full sun
Soil: well drained
Type: evergreen shrub
When to plant: cool or warm weather
Good to know: Rosemary is easy to clip into topiary forms, and you'll often find plants sold that way during the holidays. Remove the foil wrapping to ensure good drainage.

Thyme

No matter the season, thyme *(Thymus sp.)* puts on a show. Its evergreen foliage provides interest in winter and varies in color from dark green to silver to gold. In early spring, flowers open and dot the plant with white, pink, lavender, or rose. Plant lemon thyme *(T. x citriodorus)* as an edging or ground cover between paving stones, along rock walls, or in pots. Use shrublike upright common thyme *(T. vulgaris)* in borders or as small hedges.

know it, grow it

Light: full sun to partial shade
Soil: warm, light, well drained
Type: perennial
When to plant: warm weather
Good to know: Thyme can be tricky to grow from seed, so look for transplants at your local nursery or garden center. Keep soil moderately moist for best results. Restrain plants as needed by clipping back growing tips.

Rosemary

Homegrown Fruit

For a delicious taste of the season, you can't beat these plants. These garden superstars not only produce bountiful crops, but many fruiting plants flaunt flowers that match the eye-catching glory of the harvest

Blueberries

Add fruit plants to your yard this year, and get a deliciously sweet reward.

There are several good reasons to grow fruit. First, store-bought fruits are often picked, shipped, and sold before they are fully ripe. Second, stores generally stock selections that look pretty but don't necessarily taste the best. Finally, some fruits such as blueberries and figs make outstanding ornamental plants in the landscape.

Strawberries

Critter control. Animals love fruit as much as we do. Birds are especially attracted to berries. Hang reflective tape in the bushes or cover them with nylon netting. Hungry deer can eat most of a harvest in a few hours. Electric fencing, motion-activated sprinklers, commercial deer repellents, and 6- to 8-foot fencing work well for them. Stop both rabbits and raccoons with wire-mesh fencing. Tree squirrels feed on fruits, nuts, and vegetables. Protect berry vines, ripening fruits, and tomato plants with bird netting.

Blueberries

Blueberries are hard to beat. Beautiful white or pinkish flowers emerge in early spring, followed by elegant blue to green leaves. Because the colorful berries don't ripen at once, you'll see a multicolored display of green, pink, and blue. When fall rolls around, the leaves turn brilliant hues of red, yellow, and orange. Plant in full sun for the most fruit. Blueberry bushes prefer slightly moist, well-drained, acid (pH 4.5 to 5.5) soil rich in organic matter such as composted manure, chopped leaves, or peat. Position each bush with the top half-inch of the root ball resting above the surrounding soil. Rabbiteye blueberry (*Vaccinium ashei*) selections do well in the Middle, Lower, and Coastal South. Choose Northern highbush (*V. corymbosum*) selections in the Upper and Middle South.
Choose two or more selections for optimal pollination and lots of fruit.

our picks

Rabbiteye Selections	Season
'Austin'	Early
'Brightwell'	Mid
'Climax'	Early
'Powderblue'	Mid
'Premier'	Early
'Tifblue'	Mid to Late

Northern Highbush Selections	Season
'Bluecrop'	Mid
'Darrow'	Late
'Jersey'	Late
'Patriot'	Mid

know it, grow it

Light: full sun
Soil: slightly moist, well drained, acid (pH 4.5 to 5.5)
Spacing: 4 to 5 feet apart
Where to grow: everywhere except the Tropical South
Good to know: Plants often produce so many fruit buds that berries are undersized and plant growth slows down. Pruning will prevent overbearing. Keep first-year plants from bearing by stripping off flowers; on older plants, cut back ends of twigs until fruit buds are widely spaced. Or simply remove some of the oldest branches each year.

Blackberries

Newer, large-fruiting selections of this Southern favorite have made it a very desirable addition to the home garden. Thornless types such as 'Arapaho' and 'Apache' offer large fruit on upright plants that won't scratch you while you're harvesting. 'Kiowa' is a large-fruiting selection with thorny stems. Train blackberries on a fence, trellis, or wall so they will have room to climb, and you won't have to stoop over to pick them. Blackberry canes are biennial—they grow the first year, flower and fruit the second, and then die. Dead canes can harbor disease, so prune and discard any fruiting canes to the ground as soon as you finish picking the berries. New canes will soon replace them.

Blackberries

know it, grow it

Light: full sun

Soil: rich, well drained

Spacing: 4 to 5 feet apart

Where to grow: everywhere except the Tropical South

Good to know: The more sun blackberry plants receive, the more fruit they will produce. A family of four will need to grow only five or six plants to have plenty of fresh produce. The fruit is loaded with vitamin C and full of antioxidants.

Our picks: 'Arapaho,' 'Apache,' and 'Kiowa.'

Figs

With their tropical-looking leaves and stout trunks, fig trees make picturesque additions to the yard. Even better, they require very little attention. Figs are self-pollinating, so you need only one to get fruit. If you live in the Upper South, grow fig trees in containers and bring them indoors for winter. In the Middle South, fig trees may die to the ground following cold winters but then will resprout. They are hardy in the Lower, Coastal, and Tropical South.

know it, grow it

Light: partial to full sun
Soil: any well drained
Spacing: 15 to 30 feet apart, depending on selection
Where to grow: Middle, Lower, Coastal, and Tropical South
Good to know: In most areas, figs will yield a small early harvest on the previous year's growth as well as a later, bigger harvest on the new summer growth.
Our picks: 'Celeste,' 'Brown Turkey,' and

Muscadines

These native Southern grapes bear large fruit in small clusters and are the perfect fruit for the backyard gardener. Muscadines can handle the heat and humidity of the South without succumbing to diseases and pests that typically stunt other grapevines. It's very important to provide adequate moisture during the first year. Once established, muscadines are quite drought tolerant. Mulching with 2 inches of pine bark will help preserve moisture and keep roots cool. There are two kinds of muscadines: self-fertile types, which are self-pollinating, and self-sterile (female) types, which must be planted near self-fertile types to bear fruit. Start with these two selections planted together to create your own personal vineyard: 'Darlene' (female) is bronze and sweet and produces large fruit; 'Nesbitt' (self-fertile) is a very productive black grape that has outstanding flavor.

Muscadines

know it, grow it

Light: full sun

Soil: well drained (pH 6 to 6.5)

Spacing: 20 feet apart

Where to grow: everywhere except the Tropical South

Good to know: Plant container-grown or bare-root plants from late November through early March for maximum first-year development. Feed with a balanced fertilizer (10-10-10) in early spring and again in early summer. If you notice yellowing leaves, apply Epsom salts (magnesium sulfate) in the summer. Spray muscadines with fungicide periodically to keep diseases in check. The lighter the skin of the fruit, the more susceptible it is to fruit rot. If you don't want to spray, choose one of the purple selections, which are less prone to disease.

Our picks: Plant 'Darlene' (female) with 'Nesbitt' (self-fertile).

Muscadines

Strawberries

Choose from two types of strawberries: June-bearing and everbearing. June-bearing types produce one crop per year in late spring or early summer and generally are the highest-quality strawberries you can grow. Everbearing put out fewer runners than June-bearers and set fruit over a longer season. Their harvest peaks in summer and continues (often unevenly) through fall. In the Coastal and Tropical South, set out June-bearers in fall for a spring crop. Elsewhere, plant in early spring for harvest the following year. Set out everbearing plants in spring for summer-to-fall berries. Pinch off the earliest blossoms to increase plant vigor.

know it, grow it

Light: full sun
Soil: well drained
Spacing: 1 foot apart, in rows that are 2 to 2½ feet apart.
Where to grow: all regions
Good to know: Plants need about 1 inch of water per week in growing season, more when bearing fruit. Drip irrigation is ideal to help reduce disease problems. Harvest strawberries when they are fully red. They'll continue to ripen and soften for several days afterward.
Our picks: 'Allstar,' 'Earliglow,' 'Sunrise' (June-bearing). 'Ozark Beauty,' 'Tribute,' 'Selva' (everbearing).

Apples

Light: full sun
Soil: moist, fertile, well drained
Size: up to 25 feet tall and wide depending on selection.
Where to grow: everywhere but Tropical South
Good to know: You can buy three different sizes: standard (matures at 20 to 25 feet tall and wide), semi-dwarf (10 to 20 feet), and dwarf (5 to 8 feet). Dwarf and semi-dwarf are good choices for most people; they take up less room, bear fruit at a young age, and are easy to reach for harvesting and pruning. Even commercial growers favor these smaller trees.
Our picks: 'Granny Smith' (early midseason, tart, firm fruit), 'Anna' (early fruit, low chill, reliable bearer), 'Grimes Golden' (self-pollinating, midseason fruit), 'Golden Delicious,' (self-pollinating, late midseason fruit), 'Fuji' (late season fruit, stores well). For a comprehensive list, see *The Southern Living Garden Book*.

Apples

The most widely adapted deciduous fruit tree, apples grow from central Florida all the way up to Canada. Fruit ripens from June to early November, depending on type. Most selections require between 900 and 1,200 hours of 45°F or lower temperature to set fruit; if you live in the Coastal South, it's important to choose types with low winter-chill requirements. Self-pollinating selections, such as 'Golden Delicious,' will bear fruit without having another apple tree around. But most selections need cross-pollination with a different selection. If you're short on space, buy a multi-selection tree, which will have up to five types grafted onto a single trunk and rootstock, providing a variety of selections and pollination in a single tree. Trees need regular moisture while fruit is developing. Make up for lack of rainfall with periodic deep soakings.

Apples

Peaches

One of the most iconic fruits of the South, peaches are well-adapted to our dry, hot summers and chilly winters. But keep in mind that they are not low-maintenance trees. They require good drainage, a regular fertilization program, and heavier pruning than other fruit trees. When planting a bare-root tree that is unbranched, cut it back to 2 to 3½ feet above the ground (the thicker the trunk, the less severe the cutting back). New branches will form below the cut. After the first year's growth, select three well-formed branches for scaffold limbs. Remove all other branches. On mature trees, in each dormant season, cut off two-thirds of the previous year's growth by removing two of every three branches formed that year. Peaches are plagued by disease, so if you are opposed to spraying, you may want to reconsider. If you still want to try your hand at them, start with a genetic dwarf selection, such as 'Bonanza,' that can be easily reached for pruning and spraying, as they rarely reach over 7 feet tall.

know it, grow it

Light: full sun

Soil: well drained

Size: up to 25 feet tall and wide

Where to grow: everywhere, as long as you choose selections adapted to your zone

Good to know: Even with good pruning, peaches tend to set too much fruit. When fruit is about 1 inch wide, remove some of the excess so that fruit is 8 to 10 inches apart.

Our picks: 'Bonanza' dwarf. If you live in an area that has mild winters, try a low-chill selection such as 'Gold Prince' or 'Flordaprince.'

the lowdown on growing ...

Veggies

Follow these basic tips, so you'll keep on liking your homegrown vegetables.

1. Pick the right site. Leafy vegetables, such as lettuce and spinach, can usually get by with a half-day of sun. Everything else wants full sun. The more sun they get, the more produce you'll get.

2. Prepare the soil before planting. Vegetables like fertile, moist, well-drained soil that contains lots of organic matter, such as composted manure and decomposed leaves. The more you add, the better your crops will grow, and the less damage they'll suffer from insects and disease.

3. Don't plant more than you can eat, especially high producers such as tomatoes and squash. But if you do, donate the excess to a local food bank.

4. Vegetable gardens are high-maintenance propositions. They need regular watering, weeding, fertilizing, mulching, and harvesting. So if this is your first garden, start small. You can always make it bigger later.

Fruits

Homegrown fruit tastes better than what you can buy in stores. Remember the following pointers:

1. Fruits like full sun. They use sunlight to produce sugars and a sweeter taste. They also flower more in sun. More flowers mean more fruit.

2. Know the soil a particular fruit likes. Some, such as blueberries, need highly acid soil. More adaptable fruits include figs, grapes, and apples. Good drainage is essential for almost all fruits.

3. Plant selections suited to your climate zone. Ask a nurseryman or consult *The Southern Living Garden Book.*

4. Some fruits, such as figs and blackberries, are self-pollinating. But most need cross-pollination with another selection to bear fruit. Plant at least two different kinds.

5. People aren't the only creatures who love fresh fruit. If you're the only one in the neighborhood with fruit trees and bushes, the birds, squirrels, raccoons, and deer will soon find out and spread the word. Accept it.

Herbs

Herbs are doubly valuable to a garden because they offer both culinary and ornamental benefits. The following guidelines will help you succeed in growing them.

1. Herbs absolutely must have two things: full sun and excellent drainage. If you can't supply both, don't grow herbs.

2. Go easy on water and fertilizer. Herbs prefer somewhat lean and dry soil. Feeding and watering too much will water down their flavor.

3. Some herbs are annual (die in winter), while others are perennial (come back year after year). Plan for this, so you won't be surprised.

4. Herbs don't mind crowded roots. This means you can grow a wide variety of them in a relatively small space. Grow them in small planting beds or in pots.

5. When cooking with herbs, remember dried herbs have stronger flavor than fresh-picked ones.

gardening step-by-step

Success in gardening, as in any other endeavor, involves a good understanding of basic principles and procedures. Discover the fundamental information and step-by-step instructions you'll need to plant and care for your garden.

Planting Techniques

Proper planting techniques depend on the plant and how it is sold.

Planting bare-root shrubs and trees

Bare-root plants are sold in late winter and early spring. Many deciduous plants are available this way, including fruit and shade trees, flowering shrubs, roses, grapes, and cane fruits. They usually establish more quickly and grow better initially than container plants.

Select bare-root plants with strong stems and fresh-looking, well-formed roots. Avoid any with slimy roots or dry, withered ones; also reject any that have already leafed out.

Plant bare-root plants as soon as possible after purchase. If bad weather prevents immediate planting, heel in the plants by laying them temporarily in a trench dug in a shady spot in the garden and covering the roots with moist soil or potting mix; it's important not to let the roots dry out. Before planting, soak the roots for a minimum of 4 hours (or preferably overnight) in a bucket of water. Just before planting, be sure to cut any broken or damaged roots back to healthy tissue.

Planting balled-and-burlapped shrubs and trees

Some woody plants have root systems that won't survive bare-root transplanting; others are evergreen and cannot be sold bare-root. Such plants are dug from the field with a ball of soil around their roots, and the soil ball is then wrapped in burlap or a synthetic material and tied with twine or wire. These are called balled-and-burlapped (B-and-B) plants.

Select B-and-B plants with healthy foliage and an even branching structure. The covering should be intact (so that the roots are not exposed), and the root ball should feel firm and moist.

B-and-B plants can be damaged if handled roughly. Support the bottom of the root ball when moving the plant; don't pick the plant up by the trunk or drop it, which might shatter the root ball. B-and-B plants are usually quite heavy; have the nursery deliver them or have a friend help you move them in a sling of stout canvas. Once home, you can move the plant by sliding it onto a piece of plywood and pulling it to the planting spot.

Planting plants from containers

Most of the broad-leaved evergreen shrubs and trees that are the South's landscaping favorites are only offered in containers. You can buy them throughout the growing season, choosing from a variety of sizes and prices. They're relatively easy to transport, and they needn't be planted immediately.

Select container-grown plants with healthy foliage and strong shoots. Check the leaves and stems to be sure no insects are present. Avoid root-bound plants. Two common signs of this condition are roots protruding above the container's soil level and husky roots growing through the drainage holes; additional indicators are plants that are large for the size of the container, leggy plants, and dead twigs or branches.

planting 101

Bare-Root Plants

1. Make a firm cone of soil in the planting hole. Spread the roots over the cone, positioning the plant at the same depth as (or slightly higher than) it was in the growing field. Use a shovel handle or yardstick to check the depth.

2. Hold the plant upright as you firm soil around its roots. When almost complete, add water. This eliminates any air pockets. If the plant settles below the level of the surrounding soil, pump it up and down while soil is saturated to raise it to the proper level.

3. Finish filling the hole with soil; then water again. Take care not to overwater while the plant is still dormant. When the growing season begins, make a ridge of soil around the planting site to form a watering basin; water when the top 2 inches of soil are dry.

Balled-and-Burlapped Plants

1. Measure the root ball from top to bottom. The planting hole should be a bit shallower than this distance, so that the top of the root ball is about 2 inches above the soil. Adjust the hole to the proper depth; then set in the plant.

2. Untie the covering. If it's burlap, it will eventually rot; spread it out to uncover about half the root ball. If it's synthetic, however, remove it entirely. Drive a stake in alongside the root ball. Fill the hole with soil to within 4 inches of the top and water gently.

3. Firm the soil as you fill the hole. Make a berm of soil to form a watering basin; water the plant. Cover with mulch. If you staked the plant, loosely tie it to the stake. As it becomes established, keep the soil moist but not soggy. Remove the stake after the first growing season.

Container Plants

1. Dig a hole as shown above. Spread roots out over the central plateau of firm soil. The top of the root ball should be 1 to 2 inches above the surrounding soil.

2. Backfill with the unamended soil you dug from the hole, adding the soil in stages and firming it around the roots with your hands as you work.

3. Make a berm of soil to form a watering basin. Irrigate gently. Spread a layer of mulch on top of the root ball, but take care not to mound it up against the trunk.

Watering Wisely

A number of interrelated factors—including soil texture, the particular plants and their ages and root depths, and the weather—determine how much water your plants need and how often they need it.

Soil texture. Clay soils absorb water slowly and also drain slowly. Sandy soils absorb water quickly and drain just as rapidly. To improve absorption and drainage in clay and to make sandy soils more moisture retentive, work in organic amendments.

Plant maturity. Once their roots are established, different plants have widely differing watering needs. Young plants need more frequent watering than mature ones until their root systems become well established. Many annuals and vegetables require regular moisture throughout the growing season if they are to bloom well or produce a good crop.

Watering Methods

Methods for applying water range from simple handheld sprayers and hose-end sprinklers to more complex underground rigid-pipe and drip systems. The method or methods appropriate for your garden depend on how often you need to water, the size of your garden, and how much equipment you want to buy.

Hand watering. This method is useful for new transplants, seedlings, and container plants because you can apply the water gently and exactly where it's needed.

Sprinklers. Water can be applied through sprinklers attached to the end of a hose or via an inground sprinkler system. In either case, the sprinklers apply a high volume of water over a large surface area. Sprinkling does have some negative aspects. It can be wasteful. In humid climates, sprinkling encourages foliage diseases, such as black spot and powdery mildew—though you can minimize this by sprinkling early in the morning so that leaves dry as the day warms.

When selecting a sprinkler, look for one with a coverage pattern that most closely matches the area to be irrigated.

Root irrigators. These devices—which resemble giant hypodermic needles—are useful for getting water to root zones of trees growing near sidewalks, patios, or other areas with minimum open soil. Attach the tool to the end of a garden hose; then insert it into the ground as you turn the water on. Water travels down a hollow probe and shoots out of holes at the tip.

Soaking. This is an effective way to supply sufficient water to the roots of plants. For vegetables or flowers growing in rows, you can build adjoining basins for large plants or make furrows between rows. Construct the furrows when the plants are young, before their root systems have spread.

Soil soaker hoses. These are useful for a slow, steady delivery of water. They are long tubes made of perforated or porous plastic or rubber with hose fittings at one or both ends. When you attach a soaker to a regular hose and turn on the water supply, water seeps or sprinkles from the soaker along its entire length. You'll need to leave soakers on longer than you would sprinklers; to determine timing, check water penetration with a trowel or soil sampling tube.

Drip irrigation. This describes the application of water by drip emitters and microsprays. Both devices operate at low pressure and deliver a low volume of water compared to standard sprinklers. Because the water is applied slowly on or near the ground, there should be no waste from the runoff and little or no loss to evaporation. Position the emitters to deliver water just where plants need it; control penetration by varying the time the system runs and/or the emitters' delivery capacity.

You can tailor them to water individual plants by providing each with its own emitter, or distribute water over larger areas with microsprays.

Mulch

Mulching is the practice of applying organic
or inorganic materials to the surface of the soil
and around plants. Mulches help hold moisture
in the soil and insulate it from extreme or rapid
changes of temperature. They prevent most weed
seedlings from becoming established; keep mud
from splashing up onto foliage, flowers, fruit,
and surfaces; help prevent erosion; and make
your garden beds look tidy. Before applying any
mulch, clear away existing weeds.

Inorganic mulches. These include gravel and other kinds of rock, plastic sheeting, and landscape fabrics. Stones make permanent mulches that can discourage weeds effectively. Plastic warms the soil, and black plastic suppresses weeds. Landscape fabrics are porous, allowing air, water, and dissolved nutrients to reach the soil. They are best used in permanent plantings around trees and shrubs; they aren't really suited for beds of vegetables or annuals, where you change plants often. After installation, cover the fabric with a 2- to 3-inch layer of a weed-free organic mulch.

Organic mulches. Derived from once-living matter, organic mulches break down slowly, improving the soil and adding nutrients as they decompose. Choices include chopped leaves, compost, grass clippings, pine needles, shredded ground bark, wood chips, and straw. One of the most common misconceptions about mulch is that it should be applied seasonally or annually, regardless of whether or not the previous layer has decomposed. Over time, accumulated mulch can injure or kill the very plants it was put there to help. A blanket of mulch that is too thick will retard the passage of air and water and may produce harmful chemical compounds.

Allow the existing layer of mulch to decompose before applying the next. Mulch will decompose at different rates. Apply mulches in a 2- to 4-inch-thick layer on paths and around plants. Don't pile mulch against tree trunks or over a plant's crown, as this can encourage insects and rot.

good measure

Bulk quantities of organic mulch are sold by the cubic yard. Determine how many square feet you want to cover (multiply the area's length by its width), then consult the chart below to determine the appropriate amount of mulch you need.

How much mulch to use

To cover this area	2 inches deep	3 inches deep	4 inches deep
100 square feet	⅔ cubic yard	1 cubic yard	1⅓ cubic yards
250	1⅔	2½	3⅓
500	3⅓	5	6⅓
1,000	6⅔	10	13⅓

Know Your Soil

The first step to having happy, healthy plants is learning to determine the type of soil you have. Soils are divided into three basic types: sand, clay, and silt.

Sandy soil has large particles that allow water and nutrients to drain quickly. Because sandy soil is loose and easy to work, it doesn't need frequent tilling. Instead it should have generous applications of compost worked into it and a heavy layer of mulch to prevent excess water loss.

Crepe myrtle

Clay soil has tiny particles that bind tightly together and prevent water from escaping. Clay soil needs tilling to break up the hard clumps. Incorporating lots of organic matter will improve its drainage.

Silt soil has medium particles. If you're fortunate enough to have silt, the only thing you need to do is add compost to ensure an adequate supply of nutrients.

Generally, gardeners are looking for a soil that combines all three types, known as "loam." If you're unsure of what's in your yard, fill up a pot with the soil, and pour water on top. If the water percolates quickly to the bottom, you probably have sandy soil. If the water pools on top and takes more than a few minutes to penetrate the soil, it's likely you have clay soil. Silt will allow some water to penetrate immediately.

Test the pH of your soil. Another way to get to know your soil is to test the pH. This simple test will tell you if the soil tends to be acid or alkaline. You can either buy a test kit or send a soil sample to a county extension agent for testing. Either way, the results will enable you to get plants that naturally fit into your yard or show you how to slowly alter your soil.

Soil pH ranges from 0 to 14, with the higher numbers being more alkaline and the lower numbers being more acid. A soil pH of 7 is neutral, and many plants thrive at or near neutral. However, there are some notable exceptions. Azaleas, hollies, and dogwoods prefer slightly acid soil, while bougainvillea, lilacs, grapes, and figs tend to grow better in alkaline soil (a pH between 7 and 8).

There are some methods that can slowly alter a soil's pH or at least temporarily influence it. Try adding lime or gypsum to acid soil. For alkaline soil, add sulfur and chelates according to the soil test recommendations. However, a better remedy for getting around your soil's pH is to build raised beds and import new soil.

Camellia

soil problems

Some soil problems that result in poor plant growth may be due to factors other than basic soil texture. Here are a few of the most common such problems—and ways to deal with them.

Poor drainage. For most plants good drainage is essential for healthy growth. If the soil drains poorly, water remains in the pore spaces rather than draining away, and air, necessary both to roots and beneficial soil-dwelling organisms, is thus unable to enter the soil. Poor drainage may also occur naturally in the garden's low spots. Solving the problem may require installing drainage tiles to carry away excess water.

Hardpan. This is an impervious layer of soil that can cause trouble when it lies near the surface. Hardpan is found naturally in some regions. It can also be created, as when builders spread excavated subsoil over the soil surface and then repeatedly drive heavy equipment over it.

If the hardpan layer is thin and close to the surface, it may be possible to break it up by having the soil plowed to a depth of 1 foot or more. If the hardpan is thicker, you may be able to drill through the hardpan with a soil auger when planting, creating a drainage chimney. Thick hardpan, however, may require the installation of a subsurface drainage system, a project that usually requires hiring a contractor. Growing plants in raised beds filled with good soil is another alternative.

Proper Fertilization

When it comes to plant nutrition, three elements are regarded as the fundamental building blocks. Nitrogen, phosphorus, and potassium are known as "the big three" of gardening and are represented by the symbols N, P, and K. Most fertilizers contain some amount of each of these elements, and the percentages of each are always presented in that same order on the three-digit designation of the package. For example, a 5-10-3 fertilizer is 5% nitrogen, 10% phosphorus, and 3% potassium.

Nitrogen is the quick-fix element for your plants. Fertilizers high in nitrogen content spur fast growth of stems and leaves. Nitrogen is very soluble and moves through the soil easily, especially in sandy soils. Manure, cottonseed meal, and blood meal are organic nitrogen fertilizer options. It's important to add nitrogen in the spring, when your plants are beginning their growth spurt, but don't apply when new growth may be damaged by coming frost.

Phosphorus is important for root growth, as well as setting flowers and fruit. This element moves through the soil very slowly, especially in heavy clay soils, so it's best to add bloom booster directly into the planting hole, or at least use a hand cultivator to scratch it into the soil where roots can reach it. Try bonemeal for an organic alternative.

Potassium adds general vigor to your plants to help ward off disease and strengthen cold hardiness. Kelp and fish meal are good sources for potassium. Potassium also moves out of the soil, but one application per growing season is usually adequate.

Natural or Chemical?

Visit almost any nursery and you'll encounter a bewildering array of fertilizers in different forms and formulas. To decide which ones to buy, start by reading the labels.

Natural and chemical fertilizers. You can buy fertilizers in either natural (organic) or synthetic (chemical) form.

Natural fertilizers, derived from dead or living organisms, include fish emulsion, all kinds of animal manures including bat and seabird guano, and meals made from blood, bone, fish, alfalfa, cottonseed, and soybeans. Most contain lower levels of nutrients than do chemical products. Rather than dissolving in water, they are broken down by microorganisms in the soil, providing nutrients as they decay (decomposition proceeds more quickly in warm, moist soils than in cold or dry ones). Thanks to this slow nutrient release, natural fertilizers are much less likely to burn roots than are chemical types.

Many natural fertilizers are high in just one major nutrient. Some manufacturers combine several natural fertilizers in a single package to produce a complete fertilizer.

Chemical fertilizers are derived from the chemical sources listed on the product label. Compared with natural fertilizers, they usually provide higher levels of nutrients and are faster acting. They're a good choice for greening up lawns in spring and giving plants suffering from nutrient deficiencies a quick tonic. Keep in mind that chemical products can burn roots if applied too heavily.

Liquids or Solids?

Both natural and chemical fertilizers are sold in liquid and solid forms.

Liquid fertilizers, including fish emulsion and water-soluble crystals, deliver nutrients to the roots immediately. Liquid fertilizers must be reapplied frequently because their nutrients leach through the root zone rapidly.

Solid fertilizers are usually sold as powders, granules, or pellets. Solid fertilizers can be broadcast or spread over lawns and ground covers, scratched or dug into the soil around other plants, and dug into the soil when preparing new planting beds.

Other solids include controlled-release fertilizers, sold as spikes, tablets, or beadlike granules that release nutrients gradually over a fairly long period—typically 3 to 9 months—if the soil receives regular moisture.

Special-purpose fertilizers. High-nitrogen blends (such as 29-3-4) help keep lawns green and growing quickly, while higher-phosphorus mixes (6-10-4, for example) are intended to promote flowering and fruiting.

Those designed for acid lovers such as camellias, rhododendrons, and azaleas are especially useful, as are fertilizers for citrus. Another special kind of fertilizer is foliar fertilizer. These liquids are applied to leaves, which can absorb nutrients through small openings in leaves. Some solutions are high in macronutrients, while others offer an effective way to apply micronutrients.

Why Prune?

Here are a few reasons you need to prune.

To maintain the health of your plants.
Remove branches that are badly diseased, dead, or rubbing together. Plants that have become too densely branched should be thinned to allow air and sunlight to reach their inner leaves and stems, helping to discourage some diseases.

To direct growth. Each time you make a pruning cut, you stop growth in one direction and encourage it in another because growth continues in the buds and branches left behind.

To remove undesirable growth. Prune out wayward branches and remove suckers (stems growing up from the roots) and water sprouts (upright shoots growing from the trunk and branches).

To increase quality or yield of flowers or fruit. Most fruit trees and many flowering trees and shrubs need regular pruning to produce a good annual crop of fruit or blossoms.

To maintain safety. Remove split or broken branches that threaten to fall. Prune branches that obscure oncoming traffic from view.

To create hedges, topiaries, or espalier. Suitable plants can be shaped into topiaries or maintained as hedges through regular shearing.

When to Prune

In general, pruning is best done in late winter (when plants are dormant) or during mid- to late summer. Dead or badly diseased wood is an exception and should be removed as soon as you notice it. The best time to prune also depends in part on whether the plant is deciduous or evergreen.

Deciduous trees and shrubs are typically pruned in late winter or early spring, just before or just as they resume growth. To avoid cold damage to exposed tissues, prune after the danger of heavy frost is past. (Maples and birches should be pruned in summer, as they "bleed" sap if pruned in winter or spring.)

Flowering trees and shrubs are pruned based on whether they bloom on old or new wood. Plants that bear flowers in spring on wood that grew the preceding year should be pruned only after the flowering season is finished; if you prune earlier, you'll eliminate the flower buds. Woody plants that produce flowers later in the growing season on the current season's growth, however, can be pruned in late winter without sacrificing blossoms because the new (flowering) wood will grow after pruning.

Broad-leaved evergreen trees and shrubs don't drop their foliage, but growth slows down during the coldest time of year. Most can be pruned during this dormant period (late winter or early spring) or in summer. For flowering broad-leaved evergreens, you'll need to preserve flower buds. For evergreens flowering on last season's growth, prune after bloom; for those that bloom on new wood, prune before spring growth begins.

Conifers, in many cases, don't require any pruning. For those that do, timing depends on the growth habit of the conifer in question. Fir, spruce, and most pines should be pruned in early spring because they produce all their new growth in spring, with buds appearing at the tips of new shoots as well as along their length and at their bases. Random-branching conifers grow in spurts throughout the growing season rather than just in spring, though the best time for the job is usually right before spring growth begins.

pruning 101

Thinning. Most of the cuts you make when pruning should be thinning cuts. Such cuts direct growth, eliminate competing or old stems, reduce overall size, and open up a plant's structure.

Heading. These cuts remove part of a stem or branch. Heading stimulates the growth of lateral buds just below the cut. For maintenance of pruning of most woody plants, heading is less desirable than thinning. Continual heading ruins the natural shape. It is useful when your goal is to induce vigorous growth beneath a cut; force branching at a particular point on a branch or stem to train young fruit trees; fill a hole in the tree's crown; increase bloom production in roses; or rejuvenate neglected shrubs.

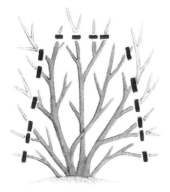

Shearing. An indiscriminate form of heading, shearing does not involve careful, precise cutting just above a growing point. Instead, you simply clip a plant's outer foliage to create an even surface, as in hedges or topiaries.

Pruning cuts. This is the simplest type of pruning. Using your thumb and forefinger or a pair of hand shears, nip off the tips of new growth, removing the terminal bud. This stops the shoot from growing longer and stimulates branching. Pinching is used primarily on annuals and perennials to make them more bushy and encourage the production of more flowers.

thinning   heading   pinching

A Few Thoughts for Success

Gardening needn't be an intimidating endeavor. Don't be frustrated by trying new things each season. In time, you'll be an expert yourself. Start here and impress your friends with your success. It will be contagious.

Edge your lawn. Most grasses can quickly escape their confines and grow into your flowerbeds. So once or twice a year, use a flat shovel to cut a clean trench 3 or 4 inches deep along the perimeter of your turf. Each time you mow, run a string trimmer along the edge to maintain your boundary.

Root a cutting. New gardeners are sometimes afraid to attempt to root a plant, but some plants are easy. Try coleus. These colorful annuals root in water with little effort. Using scissors, take a 3- or 4-inch cutting. Remove some of the lower leaves so you have about 2 inches of stem. Place it in a clear glass; in a couple of days you will notice small white bulges on the stem. Over time, these will become elongated, and roots will appear. Keep your plant in the glass, or transplant it to a container filled with soil. Once your plant has settled into the pot, plant it in a border.

Zap those weeds. Dandelions, clover, and other broad-leaved lawn weeds may have you reaching for weed-and-feed fertilizers. For these products to work effectively, the particles must stick to the foliage of the weeds for at least 24 hours. This gives the leaves enough time to absorb the herbicide and carry it down to the root. So before you apply weed-and-feed, make sure the lawn is wet, either by rain, dew, or sprinkler. Choose a product with the smallest granules you can find. The smaller they are, the better they'll stick. Don't apply weed-and-feed products when rain is expected within a day. If water washes the weed killer into the soil too soon, it won't work.

Nursery knowledge. Look at plants when they are blooming, and buy them when they're not; but if you're buying lots of one kind of azalea or crepe myrtle, buy them all in bloom. That way you won't be stuck with 14 red plants and 2 lavender ones. And always check out a nursery's guarantee and return policy before making a major plant purchase.

Plant those bulbs. Some of our best-loved garden flowers, such as daffodils and tulips, arise from bulbs. Although most familiar in dazzling spring displays, many bloom in late winter, summer, or fall and need to be planted a season ahead. Bulbs prefer rich, loose soil free from competing roots of nearby trees and shrubs, with plenty of room to send out roots of their own. A good bulb-planting trick is to first lay out all the bulbs to be planted. Then lift each one and, with a hand trowel, punch a planting hole directly beneath it. This ensures that the bulbs are evenly distributed and no gaps will appear in the daffodil display next spring. Plan for 6-inch spacing between the bulbs—that'll give a grand show for the first year and give the growing clumps enough elbow room for several more years. For a 3- x 8-foot bed, purchase 50 bulbs.

Coleus

around your garden

Discover a year's worth of tips to keep your garden in tip-top shape. Learn everything from growing and fertilizing to tools you should have. Read on and find out what you can do to keep your landscape looking great in the winter and to encourage spring blooms.

January

Grow Now: Moth Orchids

For long-lasting color inside—six weeks or more—buy moth orchids *(Phalaenopsis sp.)*. Beautiful blooms can come in yellows, purples, whites, and maroons and even have freckles or stripes. They ask only for a bright location and a planting medium that is kept slightly moist. (Orchids can be grown in soil, bark, or sphagnum moss.) Apply a diluted water-soluble fertilizer weekly. Avoid cold drafts and areas around heating vents. Gardening on a budget? Look for phalaenopsis mini orchids at your nursery.

❏ **Houseplants.** With shorter days and cooler temperatures, your inside plants are slowing down for the season. Take a break yourself, and go easy on the watering and feeding. Most houseplants like for the soil to become slightly dry between waterings.

❏ **Order seeds.** It's a great time to think about seeds for your spring vegetable and flower gardens. Buy now for the best selection.

❏ **Harvesting.** Continue to gather tasty leaves of collards and kale from your vegetable garden. The cooler weather only sweetens the flavor. Harvest regularly by pinching off the leaves from bottom up so the plants will continue to grow new ones.

vegetables

In the Lower and Coastal South, continue to harvest the heads of broccoli and cauliflower. Use clippers or a small paring knife for this task.

Grow Now: Roses

Add roses to your garden this month. Consider disease-resistant shrub types such as the editor's favorite, 'Carefree Beauty' (shown right; 3 to 5 feet, pink); 'Knock Out' (4 to 6 feet, red); 'Cramoisi Supérieur' (4 to 6 feet, red); and 'The Fairy' (2 to 3 feet, pink). Plant them en masse for best results. Climbing roses such as 'New Dawn' (pale pink), 'Cl. Cécile Brunner' (pink), and 'Rêve d'Or' (beige-yellow) need the support of a large trellis or arbor to best show off their blooms. A sunny location ensures the best blooms.

❑ Fruit plants. Purchase now for best selection. Try Southern favorites such as blackberries. 'Kiowa' is a large-fruiting selection with thorny stems. Thornless types such as 'Arapaho' and 'Apache' offer large fruit on upright plants. Other fruits include blueberries, figs, pears, muscadines, Oriental persimmons, and apples. All prefer full sun and well-drained soil.

❑ Soil prep. The mild days of winter are an ideal time for improving your soil. Work the ground when it is dry, using a garden fork to loosen the soil. Add organic matter, such as chopped leaves, composted manure, or mushroom compost to improve fertility and drainage.

forcing branches

Quince (shown right), forsythia, cherries, winter honeysuckle, and deciduous magnolias will bloom indoors with a little help. Choose stems with flowerbuds that have begun to swell. Cut stems at an angle, and place in a bucket of water. Indoors, recut stems, and place in a container of warm water with a floral preservative. Place in a cool spot in indirect light. When you begin to see color in the flowerbuds, move them to a brighter room.

March

Grow Now: Petunias and More

A bright day and a warm breeze are all it takes to make you want to get outside and plant something in your garden. The first day of spring arrives on March 20, and though it means the season has officially changed, it does not mean cold weather is over. It also may not coincide with the last frost date in your area. So what can you plant? Petunias (shown left), snapdragons, marigolds, nasturtiums, and dianthus can handle the cool days. Vegetables such as broccoli, cabbage, lettuces, kale, spinach, potatoes, and onions will do fine as well. Just wait a little longer for warm days for favorites such as caladiums, impatiens, basil, and tomatoes.

❏ **Divide now.** Perennials such as daylilies, hostas, Shasta daisies, and cannas can be divided now. Set separated plants back into the soil at the original growing depth, water well, and mulch.

❏ **Herbs.** Plant pots of thyme, rosemary, and oregano now. Wait until the danger of frost has passed before planting dill and basil.

❏ **Flowering vines.** Vines offer great solutions for color, fragrance, and shade in tight spots in the garden. They also soften fences and arbors. Try favorites such as 'Tangerine Beauty' crossvine (shown left), Carolina jessamine, and trumpet honeysuckle.

❏ **Bird's nest ferns.** Enjoy the beautiful foliage of these forgiving plants inside. 'Victoria' is a graceful kind to try. Place in a location with bright, filtered light. Water when soil feels slightly dry. Once the weather warms, you can even put it outside in a shady spot. Place it in a pot with impatiens for a colorful combination.

smart watering

Water efficiently using drip hoses. Drip irrigation applies water slowly so it can be absorbed more efficiently. Make the task even more effective by connecting the hose to a mechanical timer at your hose bib, saving water, money, and time.

Grow Now: Dogwood Trees

The beautiful spring blossoms of flowering dogwoods (*Cornus florida*) are Southern favorites. In addition to blooms, these native trees offer crimson fall foliage and bright red berries in winter. They prefer moist, acid, well-drained soil that has lots of organic matter such as peat. Try disease-resistant selections such as 'Appalachian Spring,' 'Junior Miss,' and 'Cherokee Sunset.' Dogwoods bloom well in light shade but can take more sun with additional mulch and moisture. They make perfect understory trees to fill gaps between taller trees and lower-growing shrubs. Other easy-to-grow spring blooming trees include cherry, flowering crabapple, Eastern redbud, Carolina silver bell, and fringe.

❏ **Impatiens.** These flowers will brighten shady areas until fall. Mounding masses are covered with red, rose, white, salmon, orange, and pink single or double flowers. They work great in containers or as accents in shade. Impatiens like evenly moist soil and are relatively pest free.

❏ **Mulch.** Apply a layer of mulch to newly planted trees, shrubs, and vines.

❏ **Daffodils.** Once these dependable bulbs have finished blooming, you may want to cut them back to clean up the look of your flowerbeds—but *wait!* Bulbs use these leaves to transform energy from the sun for next year's flowers. Leave them alone until their foliage turns yellow and begins to wither. Then you can pull the dried debris away with your hands.

japanese maples

It's hard to resist the elegant foliage of these graceful trees. Buy now for the best selection. Use them as specimens in your yard or in large pots on your patio. They prefer filtered light and moist, well-drained soil. Two good choices with a weeping form are 'Crimson Queen' and 'Inaba-shidare.'

May

Grow Now: Knock Out Roses

For long-lasting, easy color, plant Knock Out roses. Low maintenance and disease resistant, they love to bloom. The original 'Knock Out' rose (shown left) has cherry-red single petals. 'Pink Knock Out' has beautiful pink single petals. There are also double-flower forms of both red and pink. 'Blushing Knock Out' offers light pink blooms. The newest of the Knock Out roses is the yellow 'Sunny Knock Out.' 'Rainbow Knock Out' has a range of colors from light pink to yellow to coral with a yellow center. Plant them en masse—they make great informal hedges. They will flower best in a sunny spot (at least six hours of sun a day) with good drainage. There's no need to keep the flowers groomed; they're self-cleaning.

❏ Gift hydrangeas. Enjoy the big blossoms of potted French hydrangeas (in blue, pink, or white) inside for three to four weeks. Care is simple. Place in a cool room with bright, indirect light. Water plants regularly (check every other day), allowing the soil to dry slightly between waterings. Don't let plants sit in saucers of standing water.

❏ Choosing sod. Bermuda grass is a practical choice because it can exist on natural rainfall; however, it needs to be irrigated during periods of drought or it will go dormant. St. Augustine grass will thrive in more shade than Bermuda grass but requires more water to keep it green. Buffalo grass is a good choice for dry areas and can be interplanted with blue bonnets and other wildflowers—especially for a natural look.

taming tomatoes

As the growing season progresses, keep your tomatoes in line. Stretch tie, twine, and tomato clips all put plants on the right path. (It's okay if you have not planted yours yet; there's still plenty of time.) Try galvanized cattle panel (shown left) for solid support. Wooden tomato stakes and wire pens and cages can also help keep them inbounds.

June

Grow Now: Fragrant Gardenias

These elegant Southern pass-alongs fill the days of summer with perfume. Blossoms open white and then fade to gold. They prefer rich, well-drained, acid soil with lots of organic matter. Place them along pathways, at the corners of your house, or near windows where you can appreciate them even inside your home. If you find their fragrance too strong, locate them farther out in your yard. Most gardenias do best in the Lower, Coastal, or Tropical South. Cold-tolerant selections such as 'Heaven Scent,' 'Chuck Hayes,' 'Kleim's Hardy,' and 'Frostproof' work well in the Middle South. In the Upper South, use gardenias as potted plants outside in summer, and overwinter in a cool greenhouse.

❑ Easy houseplant. 'Neon' pothos has bold chartreuse leaves that will enliven any room. It prefers bright, indirect light. Care is simple: Let the soil dry slightly between waterings, and never let plants sit in saucers of water. Love chartreuse? Other houseplants you might try include 'Rita's Gold' Boston fern, 'Moonlight' philodendron, and 'Lemon Lime' and 'Limelight' dracaenas.

❑ Rubber hoses. Watering by hand allows you to get just the right amount of moisture to your plants. Spend a little extra money up front to buy a good hose. Rubber hoses are more durable and kink less—so you won't waste your time untangling them.

blackberries

Larger-fruiting selections have made this Southern favorite an even more appealing addition to the backyard garden. 'Kiowa' and 'Shawnee' are large-fruiting selections with thorny stems. Thornless types such as 'Apache' and 'Ouachita' offer big berries on upright plants. All prefer full sun and well-drained soil. They can be grown easily along a fence, trellis, or wall. Space plants 4 to 5 feet apart.

July

Grow Now: Blueberries

One of the simple joys of summer, blueberries are an excellent fruit for new gardeners. Northern highbush blueberries are best for the Upper and Middle South. Try selections such as 'Patriot' and 'Liberty.' Rabbiteye blueberries are best in the Lower and Coastal South. Use 'Climax' or 'Premier.' They all prefer slightly moist, well-drained, acid soil in a sunny spot. It's important to plant at least two or more selections for optimal pollination so you can have lots of fruit. Buy at your local nursery.

❏ **Butterflies.** Choose flowers that provide lots of nectar, such as salvia, penta, lantana, coneflower, verbena, and summer phlox. Add host plants for caterpillars to feed on, including parsley, dill, and milkweed. A shallow dish, filled with moist sand, offers a place for a drink. Butterflies love to bask in the sun; add a few flat rocks so they can rest between flights.

❏ **Herbs.** Cut basil, thyme, and rosemary frequently to keep these plants in full production. **Tip:** Keep a pot of your favorite herbs near your grill for a reminder (once washed) to flavor your summer meals.

❏ **Fragrance.** Add some sweet scents to your garden this season. The blooms of gardenias, ginger lilies, 'Honeybells' hostas, and tuberoses will add welcome perfume to the summer garden. Enjoy their fragrance inside by cutting a few stems for casual bouquets.

quick summer arrangements

Flowers are one of the simple joys of the season. If you don't have your own cutting garden, grab a cup of coffee and go early in the morning to your local farmers market for the best selection of bargain blooms. Summer picks include sunflowers, liatris, tithonias, and dahlias. Reflect the season's casual side by using whatever's at hand for vases. Oversize glasses, vintage graniteware pitchers, colorful tin cans, and jars all work well.

Grow Now: Tomatoes and More

Nothing is more local than your own backyard. Keep a close watch on your vegetable garden now, checking daily to gather the freshest veggies. Pick tomatoes and peppers early in the morning on the day you plan to eat them. Select cucumbers, eggplants, okra, squash, and zucchini when they are small and tender. Use sharp clippers or a small knife to harvest. Southern peas should also be picked early, as they ripen, for best flavor. Now is also the time to begin planning and planting your fall vegetable garden.

❏ Hostas. The foliage of these fine perennials will dress up any shade garden. Good ones to try include 'Blue Angel,' 'Patriot,' 'Halcyon,' and 'Guacamole.' Plant them en masse, or pair with ferns. Look for these at your local nursery.

❏ Colorful houseplants. Bromeliads are easy and offer bold foliage in cheerful, long-lasting colors. Care is casual. They prefer bright, indirect light. Allow the soil to dry slightly between waterings. Use bromeliads to perk up any room; they also work well outside on porches and shady patios.

❏ Hummingbirds. Give these beautiful winged wonders what they want—flowers! There are many blooms with nectar they love to sip. Plant pineapple sage, bee balm, Mexican bush sage, anise-scented sage, cuphea, shrimp plant, firebush (*Hamelia patens*), trumpet honeysuckle, cardinal flower, and pentas.

zinnias

Summer's most casual flowers are ideal for simple arrangements. Create easy bouquets of just zinnias (shown right), or mix them with other seasonal favorites such as gomphrenas, cosmos, sunflowers, and celosias.

September

Grow Now: Spider Lilies

The scarlet blooms of spider lilies *(Lycoris radiata)* appear, as if by magic, after the rainy days in late summer and early fall. With no foliage and no warning, spiderlike clusters of flowers spring up on 18-inch stems. After they bloom, they develop silver-centered, grassy foliage that lasts through winter and into spring. These Southern pass-alongs are grown from bulbs. They thrive on neglect, bloom in sun or shade, and will multiply in your garden. Plant in well-drained soil, and divide every four or five years in late spring as the foliage begins to turn yellow and wither.

❏ **Autumnal equinox.** September 22 marks the end of summer and the beginning of fall. It's time to set out this season's annuals, create new containers, buy bulbs, and plant trees and shrubs. (See pages 236–237 for planting tips.) Most important, just be sure to get outside and enjoy your garden and the cooler days ahead.

❏ **Plant veggies.** In the Middle, Lower, and Coastal South, begin planting your fall veggies. Set out transplants of lettuce (shown right), collards, kale, broccoli, cauliflower, cabbage, arugula, and Swiss chard. Planting on a budget? Sow seeds of lettuce, arugula, collards, beets, and radishes. No room? Plant them in pots!

❏ **Basil care.** Keep this tasty herb in full production by pinching flowers to increase the growth of new leaves.

muscadines

These sweet Southern grapes are the perfect fruit for your backyard. Plant vines this fall on a simple trellis. Start with these two types, planted together. 'Darlene' (female) is bronze and produces large fruit. 'Nesbitt' (self-pollinating) is a black grape with great flavor.

October

Grow Now: Old-Fashioned Mums

These are some of the finest perennials available for Southern gardens. Their soft colors and graceful habits steal the show in fall borders. Excellent selections include 'Hillside Sheffield' (apricot-pink; shown right), 'Cathy's Rust' (rusty peach), 'Clara Curtis' (clear pink), 'Country Girl' (rosy pink), 'Ryan's Pink' (soft pink), and 'Emperor of China' (silvery, rosy pink). Good companion plants include salvias, asters, and ornamental grasses. Look for old-fashioned mums at your local nursery.

❏ **Buy pumpkins.** Pumpkins are now available in a range of colors at grocery stores and local farmers markets. Look for ones that are firm and unblemished and have their stems still attached. Keep in a cool, dry spot to extend their use outside. No time to create a display? Just pick multiple pumpkins of the same color in different sizes to keep things simple.

❏ **Bold color.** Crotons (shown right) are beautiful houseplants that echo the shades of the season with their yellow, orange, red, and green leaves. Use them to brighten any indoor room or to dress

up an entry to your garden or home. Let the soil dry slightly between waterings.

pansies

Begin planting these happy flowers in your beds to help roots become established before colder weather sets in. Set out transplants in a sunny location in rich, well-drained soil. Use ornamental cabbages or kales as a backdrop for the blooms.

November

Grow Now: Paperwhites

With fragrant flowers and multiple blooms, paperwhites are seasonal favorites. Great for a new gardener or one with a green thumb, these bulbs are so carefree that they don't even have to be planted in soil to bloom (they can grow in pebbles or water). Start by choosing large, plump bulbs from a garden center or a mail-order source. Select a glazed pot or bowl, and fill partway with pebbles; place bulbs on pebbles. Add a few more pebbles to support bulbs. Pour in water up to the bases of the bulbs. Flowers should appear in three to six weeks. Stake, if needed (just cut bare branches from your yard). No time for all that? Buy bulbs prepotted and ready to grow. Easy—and remember, they make great gifts!

❑ **Rake leaves.** Piles of leaves can become wet blankets after rains smother your grass. Rake leaves from your lawn regularly throughout the fall, or gather them with the bagging attachment on your mower. Add the chopped leaves to shrub beds or flower beds to mulch plants and enrich your soil.

❑ **Perennials.** In the Lower and Coastal South, dig up and divide daisies, irises, and daylilies. Use a garden fork. Gently pull apart lifted plants with your hands. Set divisions back at the original growing depth, firm soil around plants, and water.

❑ **Rex begonias.** The elegant foliage of these beautiful houseplants will illuminate any room in your home. Leaf colors can come in pinks, purples, greens, and silvers (they pair perfectly with the blooms of African violets). They prefer bright, indirect light. Let the soil dry slightly between waterings.

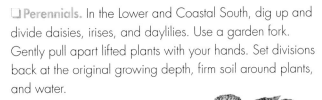

fall-blooming shrub

In the Lower and Coastal South, the blooms of the Confederate rose (*Hibiscus mutabilis*, shown left) will surprise you with their size and beauty. Flowers can be 4 to 6 inches across, opening white or pink and then turning red.

Grow Now: Rosemary Topiaries

Purchase rosemary clipped as small trees (cone-shaped) or standards (lollipop-shaped) at nurseries, garden centers, or grocery stores. The versatile herb will provide fragrance, decoration, and flavor this holiday season. Use topiaries as tabletop trees inside or in containers outside by your door. Cut as needed for cooking. Water plants regularly, letting the soil dry slightly between waterings. Never let plants sit in saucers of water. Tip: Rosemary topiaries can dry out quickly. To make watering easier, repot your plants into containers that are a little larger than the original ones. If your plants are outside, protect them from freezing weather. With a little care, you'll enjoy rosemary in your garden for years.

❑ **Mulch.** Your trees and shrubs will all appreciate a little extra protection during the winter months. After the first frost, add a 2-inch layer of pine straw or finely shredded pine bark mulch around the bases of your plants. You can also use fallen leaves. Rake them into a pile, and chop them up with your lawn mower. Then gather the leaves, and spread them around your plants.

❑ **Amaryllis.** This plant's blooms can need help standing tall. Two bamboo stakes will work well. Place a stake on each of the bulb's outside edges. Wrap twine, ribbon, or raffia around the stakes to keep the stalk straight.

❑ **Sasanquas.** Sasanqua camellias are elegant evergreens and welcome additions to any landscape. Choose the bright petals of 'Yuletide,' which blooms just in time for the holidays. Other favorites include 'Apple Blossom,' 'Chansonette,' 'Daydream,' 'Leslie Ann,' and 'White Doves.'

berries

Look for plants that provide lots of winter color for your garden. Good choices include deciduous hollies such as possumhaw *(Ilex decidua)* and winterberry *(I. verticillata)*. Other options include evergreen hollies such as American holly *(I. opaca)*, yaupon holly *(I. vomitoria)*, and selections of Chinese holly *(I. cornuta)* such as 'Burfordii,' 'Dazzler,' and 'Berries Jubilee.'

Reading the Maps

Southern Living divides the South into five broad climate zones: Upper South (US), Middle South (MS), Lower South (LS), Coastal South (CS), and Tropical South (TS). The boundaries of these zones correspond to those of the recently updated United States Department of Agriculture (USDA) Plant Hardiness Zone Map. The Upper South is in USDA Zone 6, the Middle South in Zone 7, the Lower South in Zone 8, the Coastal South in Zone 9, and the Tropical South in Zone 10. It's important to note that because the USDA map reflects minimum yearly temperatures, it functions solely as a cold-hardiness map. In the South, however, heat is as much a limiting factor as cold. Therefore, when we give a plant a *Southern Living* climate zone rating, we take into account both summer heat and winter cold. For example, if we recommend astilbe as a permanent plant for your area, we mean that it will not only survive your winters but also endure your summers, and that it will perform satisfactorily for you. We won't recommend astilbe for the Coastal or Tropical South, because although it takes winters there, in summer it melts faster than ice sculptures on a cruise ship.

Upper South (US). This region experiences the longest winters and shortest summers in the South, but summers are still hot and sticky. Fortunately, sizzling Southern temperatures rarely last long. Plants that need cool nights and long periods of winter chill do well here. Cold winters bring constraints, however. Frozen soil means that dahlias, cannas, glads, and other summer-flowering bulbs must be dug up in fall and stored over winter. Crepe myrtle, camellias, and figs may not be cold-hardy in all areas. The last frost occurs anywhere from mid-April to the first 10 days of May.

Middle South (MS). This region forms a transition zone between warm-weather and cool-weather growing zones. Here you often encounter plants from the Northeast, the Midwest, and the Northwest growing alongside Southern natives. Summers are hot and, in most places, humid. The last spring frost generally occurs in the last two weeks of April.

Lower South (LS). Spring comes early to the Lower South. Daffodils, flowering quince, and winter daphne open their buds in February. Though summer droughts are common, torrential downpours more than make up the difference. Snow is rare, but ice storms are not. The last frost generally occurs in the first

'Hella Lacy' aster: Middle South

Sweet William: Upper South

'Climbing Pinkie' rose: Lower South

Southern Living Planting Zones

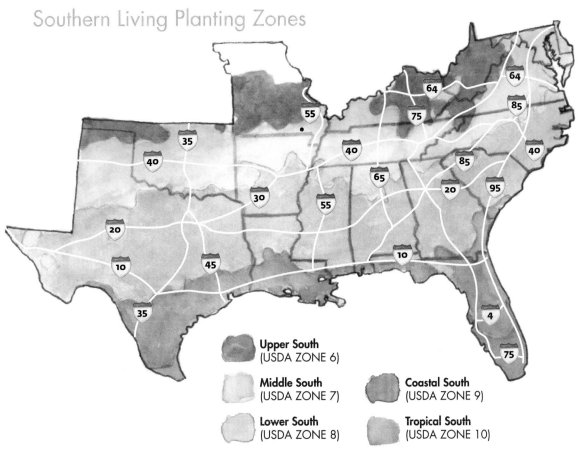

Upper South
(USDA ZONE 6)

Middle South
(USDA ZONE 7)

Lower South
(USDA ZONE 8)

Coastal South
(USDA ZONE 9)

Tropical South
(USDA ZONE 10)

Chinese fringe:
Coastal South

Gardenia:
Tropical South

two weeks of April.

Coastal South (CS). Two large bodies of water—the Atlantic Ocean and the Gulf of Mexico—rule the Coastal South. Their close proximity ensures that winters are mild and brief but summers are long and humid. The last spring frost usually comes in the second or third week in March. Spring commences in January, when the oriental magnolias and common camellias bloom.

Tropical South (TS). Truly its own gardening world, the Tropical South rarely feels frost. In fact, the lowest temperature on record for Miami is 30 degrees. Whereas most of the South deals with dry summers and wet winters, a large portion of the Tropical South reverses that pattern. All sorts of lush, exotic plants with strikingly colorful blooms and foliage flourish. To outsiders, this region can seem like a paradise. But the lack of winter chill comes at a price. Apples, azaleas, forsythia, hosta, hydrangea, and many other temperate plants fail here.

The American Horticultural Society Plant Heat Zone Map

This map divides the United States into 12 zones. Heat zones are based on the average number of days in the year that high temperatures reach or exceed 86 degrees F, the point at which plants suffer heat stress.

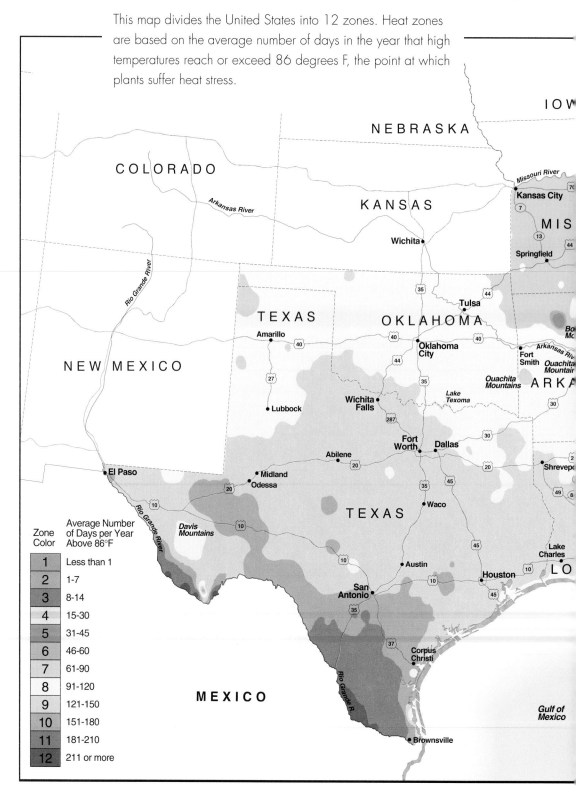

Zone Color	Average Number of Days per Year Above 86°F
1	Less than 1
2	1-7
3	8-14
4	15-30
5	31-45
6	46-60
7	61-90
8	91-120
9	121-150
10	151-180
11	181-210
12	211 or more

INDIANA   OHIO

ILLINOIS

PENNSYLVANIA

Pittsburgh
Philadelphia
Wilmington

Wheeling
Columbus
Indianapolis
Cincinnati

Delaware Bay
Dover

Cumberland
Frederick
Baltimore
DELAWARE

WEST VIRGINIA

Appalachian Mountains
Washington, D.C.
Alexandria
MARYLAND

Charleston

Chesapeake Bay

Charlottesville
Richmond

VIRGINIA

Louisville
Lexington

Virginia Beach

KENTUCKY

Lynchburg

Bowling Green

Appalachian Mountains

Winston-Salem
Durham
Greensboro
Raleigh
Greenville

Cape Girardeau

Paducah

Nashville
Knoxville
Asheville
NORTH CAROLINA

Charlotte

Memphis

TENNESSEE

Chattanooga

Appalachian Mountains
Spartanburg

Wilmington

Tupelo

Huntsville

Blue Ridge Mountains
Greenville
Columbia
SOUTH CAROLINA
Florence

Charleston

Gadsden
Atlanta
Augusta

MISSISSIPPI

Columbus

Birmingham
Anniston

Tuscaloosa

Macon
Savannah

Columbus

Jackson

Meridian

ALABAMA
Montgomery

GEORGIA

Hattiesburg

Albany

Dothan

Atlantic Ocean

Mobile

Pensacola

Jacksonville

Biloxi

Tallahassee

Lake Ponchartrain
Lake Borgne
Lake Maurepas

New Orleans

Mississippi R. The Delta

Gainesville

Lake George
Daytona Beach

Orlando

Tampa

FLORIDA

Gulf of Mexico

Fort Myers
Lake Okeechobee

Sanibel Island

Miami

The Everglades

0   50   100   150 Miles

Florida Keys

Key West

index

acknowledgements:

John & Joretta Chance,
    Lafeyette, Louisiana, p. 11
Marty & Fred Hirons, Cashiers,
    North Carolina, p. 15
Cam & Dean Williams,
    Ware Neck, Virginia, p. 21
Deborah Balter,
    Coconut Grove, Florida,
    p. 27
Sigourney Cheek,
    Nashville, Tennessee, p. 31
Will & Penelope Wright,
    Edisto Island, South Carolina,
    p. 35
Susan Hudson,
    Douglasville, Georgia, p. 41
Bill & Diane Welch,
    Central Texas, p. 47
Jon Carloftis & Dale Fisher,
    Lexington, Kentucky, p. 53
Jim Scott,
    Lake Martin, Alabama,
    p. 59